D0296757

N.N.

MICHAEL GREEN'S
RUGBY ALPHABET

MICHAEL GREEN'S
RUGBY ALPHABET

MICHAEL GREEN

Illustrated by RAY CHESTERTON

PELHAM BOOKS

First published in Great Britain by
PELHAM BOOKS LTD
52 Bedford Square
London, W.C.1
1971

© 1971 by Michael Green

sbn   7207 0403 0

Set and printed in Great Britain by
Tonbridge Printers Ltd, Peach Hall Works, Tonbridge, Kent
in Baskerville eleven on thirteen point on paper supplied by
P. F. Bingham Ltd, and bound by
Dorstel Press at Harlow

For

Stoneygate, Leicester Thursday and Ealing
Rugby Football Clubs, whose colours I regularly wore,
with apologies to the dozen other teams through whom I
passed fleetingly and disastrously

AUTHOR'S NOTE

The chapter on kicking contains some material from my
contribution to the Rugby Union Centenary Year publica-
tion *Touchdown*. As this present book is also being published in Centenary Year perhaps I can take this opportunity
to congratulate the Rugby Union and to raise my hat to the
pioneers of 100 years ago.

I always feel the sort of rugby many of us have played had
a great deal in common with the spirit of play 100 years
ago. Recently I read the history of the Leicester club, which
reveals that in 1880 a try against Market Harborough was
scored by a youth who had never played rugby, and who was
picked up outside the station. And at Kettering, Leicester
marched off the field, complaining the home team had scored
from a crooked throw-in (there was no referee). Leicester
reported, 'Kettering made it a very rough game, kicking and
scragging, which made it very unpleasant for us, who are
not used to playing that sort of game.'

If the founders of the R.U. could return today they might
find the magnificence of the great international grounds
rather frightening. But they would be pleased to find that,
despite the lapse of 100 years, players are still being picked
up at railway stations and elsewhere and given instant initia-
tion into the game. There may well be no referee; and in
moments of stress the old Blackheath custom of 'hacking'
may still be observed.

Have no fear, O Shades of the Past. The torch is in
safe hands. I wish I could say the same for the ball.

Michael Green

A is for . . .

Annual General Meeting

The Annual General Meeting of the Old Rottinghamians Rugby Union Football Club was held in the pavilion on May 31st. There were five members present when the meeting commenced at eight o'clock. This number later increased to 36 and then diminished to two.

The minutes of the previous A.G.M. were read by the secretary. A motion proposed by Mr A. Jobling that the minutes were a travesty of the proceedings, and that the secretary had remembered it all wrong, was defeated.

The chairman then gave his report. It had been, he said, another year of steady progress for this grand old club. The playing record of won 7, lost 31, drawn 3, points for 96, against 433 might have been better (cries of 'No, you're kidding, mate'). But there was more to rugby football than merely winning. Personally he did not go along with this modern emphasis on victory. The important thing was to play the game, play the gentleman and play the ball. Of course, victory was always possible by adopting such underhand methods such as coaching and tactics. The French were adept at this, and we all knew what happened to them in 1940. He was proud to say that they had boycotted the county coaching scheme.

He felt he could not conclude without a warning about the evil influences that were creeping into this grand old game of ours, helped by the sensationalism of the popular Press, although he was sorry to see that even the Daily Telegraph had now descended to criticizing that splendid body of men, the England selectors.

As an example of the evil influences, he quoted the fact that at least a third of the guests at the annual dinner failed to wear a dinner-jacket. Indeed, he had actually seen one of the younger players at a match not wearing his club tie.

People were coming into the game who would never have been allowed in the old days.

Some were demanding more competition in rugby. Others wanted to make it more interesting for the spectator. Speaking for himself, he hoped he would never live to see the day when people enjoyed watching rugby. That sort of thing should be left to professionals. Personally he felt it was all somehow tied up with sex.

A motion that the chairman's report be adopted was passed by one vote to nil, the remainder of the members being in the bar when the vote was taken.

The Hon. Treasurer then spoke at some length. While everybody had a copy of the balance sheet, he advised them not to look at it, as they wouldn't understand it. The main point was that by writing up the fixed assets and writing down the floating assets, they had turned a profit into a loss.

A member: 'Isn't that bad?'

Hon. Treasurer: 'Not necessarily. Pounds and pence are meaningless symbols. A loss might well make more money for the club than a profit.'

After several members confessed themselves baffled, the Treasurer advised the meeting to pass the accounts as printed, as he had in any case no intention of changing them now, and he would try to explain it all afterwards.

The accounts were adopted by acclamation.

Arising out of the accounts, Mr Albert Sidewinder, a founder-member of the club, asked if the money might not be saved on coaches if the first team would bicycle to away matches?

'I know times have changed since I was a wing-three-quarter, said Mr Sidewinder (cries of "Yes, they've invented the aeroplane") but I do know that when we used to play Beckenham some of us cycled over there and others actually walked, and we were none the worse for it, apart from feeling exhausted when we arrived.'

Mr Septimus Baffle then rose and said he was an even

older member than Mr Sidewinder and it was not Beckenham they walked to but Bromley. Several players even ran there and back, sometimes tying their legs together to make it more difficult.

Personally he felt the modern player was too mollycoddled. Hot baths after the game had a weakening effect. In his day, after a match they threw buckets of river water over each other and apart from the occasional case of typhoid, they were none the worse for it.

It was all a result of abolishing flogging. Personally he scourged himself twice a day and look at him now. The abolition of hanging had not helped. It would do some of these youngsters good to go down the mines.

At this point the chairman interrupted and thanked Mr Sidewinder and Mr Baffle for their interesting reminiscences, which older members had heard several times before, and declared the discussion of the accounts closed.

Mr Sidewinder: 'It would never have done for Bongo Paisley' (shouts of: 'Pipe down, you old idiot' etc. etc.).

The election of officers then took place. All nominations were unopposed, with the exception of the third team captain for which Mr J. Hardstaff and Mr F. Baker were both proposed. After a ballot, Mr Hardstaff was elected by 17 votes to nine, with eight spoilt papers. Four members who attempted to vote twice were also disqualified.

After Mr Hardstaff's election, Mr Baker rose to address the meeting. On being told that he was out of order, and in any case there was no need to stand on his chair, Mr Baker commented that everyone knew the club was run by a clique. He had given the best years of his life to the club and this was what happened. As far as he was concerned they could stuff the third team and its new captain right up the drainpipes.

Mr. Baker then adjourned to the car-park, and blew his horn for 10 minutes as a gesture of protest.

The chairman then announced any other business.

Mr. P. Pettigrew said he knew he was speaking on behalf of most of the second team when he queried the methods of team selection. Most people were convinced that the first team was picked because they all lived on the 37 bus route.

'I scored two tries against the Old Bagfordians' he declared, 'and instead of putting me up to the first they dropped me to the thirds.'

The team secretary replied that he had some sympathy with Mr. Pettigrew, but he had been dropped to the thirds because he had a car and it was an away game. He suggested that if Mr. Pettigrew really wanted promotion he should sell his car.

Mr. Pettigrew said he was flabbergasted and dumbfounded. This explanation accounted for a lot. They had better watch it or else (cries of 'Hear, hear').

After several members had complained that certain privileged people could get drinks after closing-time, the chairman declared the meeting closed. A vote of thanks to the chair failed for lack of a seconder.

A is also for . . .

Aaaaaarrrrggghhhh

Noise frequently given off by Welsh front-row forwards.

B is for . . .

One of the things I've discovered over the years, is that the quantity of kit carried by a player has nothing to do with the playing skill of its owner, and this is especially true of rugby, where the amount of equipment used seems to get less and less as one reaches higher up the scale.

International players are liable to arrive in the dressing-room at Twickenham carrying an old carrier-bag, and casually ask, 'Can anybody lend me a pair of boots, please?' But ancient no-hopers, serving out their remaining days with the Extra C, will arrive at a match with great, elephantine boxes packed with every conceivable device for their protection and comfort.

They watch over these jealously, refusing to lend anything, not so much as a piece of cotton wool, making excuses like, 'I've only enough for myself. It's all right for you

...with great elephantine boxes packed with every conceivable device ...

youngsters, but *I'm* liable to have a haemorrhage during the game.'

This vast load of baggage contains much more than the normal equipment of boots, shorts and so forth. Prominent among the additional kit will be a bottle, jar or vat of some magic potion. Older players tend to cling to this sort of thing as a miracle-talisman, swearing that its virtues will cure soreness, bruising and scratching, as well as rendering the user impervious to pain.

The magic potion may be rubbed on, rubbed in, spread around the ears, squirted elsewhere, or even swallowed. Sometimes it is a well-known brand, but usually it has an archaic title like 'Dr. Turnip's Guaranteed Muscle Invigorator and Restorative', which the player boasts can only be obtained from a small shop in Limehouse or Stepney. In rare instances, the potion may be home-made, in which case the inventor will enthusiastically offer to supply it all round the dressing-room. Do not accept the offer, as upon applying it the skin may well turn black.

Other items in the older player's box, bag or trunk might include a roll of toilet paper (there's never any in the proper place); a Rugby Union handbook which in emergencies will serve the same purpose as the toilet paper and can also be used for embarrassing the referee with awkward questions; a pyjama cord, which has a thousand uses from supporting shorts to stopping severe bleeding; and an old scrum-cap, *irrespective of whether the player is a forward or not.*

The reason for the last piece of equipment is that the moral effect of a scrum-cap worn by a threequarter is quite devastating. In most junior games all the threequarters are cowards (that is why they are in the threequarters, not because they can run fast), and they will curl up in fear at the sight of their opposite number wearing a scrum-cap, with its suggestion that the owner is really a tearaway second row man filling in with the backs.

Even with a forward, a properly prepared scrum-cap has

a great moral effect. No forward over thirty should ever set foot on the field without one. Before being used it should be carefully painted with blood. If you should write inside it 'Property of Bedford Football Club (R.U.)' and leave it before the game where the opposition will see it, so much the better.

Other items in the veteran's baggage may include a tin of cough sweets; aspirins to kill post-match headaches or pre-match hangovers; and yards of elastic bandage. This is rarely used for its proper purpose, but more often for holding together boots which have split asunder or for wrapping round the hand with the adhesive side outwards – a sure method of ensuring you will never drop another pass. It is also useful for mending leaky car exhaust pipes.

Considering rugby is supposed to be a game for the fit and the strong, it's surprising how much kit consists of medical aids more suitable to a geriatric ward. I often wonder what people who don't know the game would say if they could peer into the average dressing-room and see men injecting themselves with insulin, strapping up varicose veins or even inserting suppositories. Others might be praying.

A book of out-of-date club draw tickets is another useful item. It doesn't matter how old they are, they can be produced as a defence when pestered to buy some of the opponent's draw tickets, with the suggestion to call the transaction quits without any money passing.

Then there are personal extras to suit individual tastes. My old pal Slasher Williams always carried a complete first-aid box when appearing against teams from the Coventry area. I knew another man who always packed his guitar, in the hope that after the match everyone would ask him to play. They never did, but they filled his guitar with beer one night instead. An Irishman used to bring his bagpipes even though he couldn't play them.

The same man wouldn't play without a religious locket around his neck to give protection against evil, bad luck, referees and wing-forwards. Unfortunately it provided an ideal handle for tackling him, and frequently the game would be interrupted by a cry of, 'Ref, some blaspheming bastard has torn off me St. Simeon,' and play would be held up while we all searched in the mud.

If the locket wasn't found, play went on without Patrick, who crawled around on his hands and knees with his nose to the ground until he did find it, ignoring the complaints of players who kept tripping over him.

When St. Simeon was at last discovered there would be a great whoop of 'Now you're for it, you Protestant scum', and Patrick would rejoin the fray, usually from an offside position.

The modern habit of wearing brief trunks forbids the old custom of carrying a lot of essential kit on to the field of play itself, as one could do in the days of those long, baggy 'shorts' which finished just above the knee. No longer do player's pockets bulge with handkerchiefs and packets of lozenges.

Incidentally, it is interesting to recall that in the days of the baggy shorts we often didn't bother with a surgical support, but forwards did frequently wear shinguards. Today shinguards are unknown and supports come in all shapes, colours and sizes, an interesting example of how the emphasis on the vital part of the body has shifted in this permissive age.

Some pampered first-class sides provide all the kit a player needs. Many launder player's shirts for them. I always feel this takes some of the individuality out of rugby, because a man's potential can often be summed up by the condition of his kit.

My own experience has been that the man with the knife-edge crease in his shorts, and immaculate linen, was almost always an exhibitionist coward. The player to be careful of was the one stumbling about with an arm of his jersey tied on with a shoelace.

For a bachelor, looking after kit is an almost impossible

task. If he doesn't wash it he can hardly move the following Saturday (I'm sure this is the real reason for the poor standard of running in most of the lower sides). On the other hand, any attempt to wash it at the Laundromat blocks drains for miles around. I once caused a complete battery of washing-machines to break down in a suburban Bendix, through washing mud-caked rugby kit. The fact that I put my boots in as well may have had something to do with it.

Incidentally, never mix ordinary clothes with the rugby washing unless you wish to have underwear in your club colours for the rest of the season.

Warning should be taken from the experience of my old friend Taffy Owen, whose girl-friend washed his kit one Friday night in February, and hung it on the line to dry. When Taffy arrived to collect it in a hurry just before the game it had frozen solid, including his jock-strap, which resembled a Henry Moore sculpture. It was the only occasion on which I have seen a player arrive and stand his jersey in the corner of the dressing-room.

C is for . . .

Captain

During a game of rugby one of the players may be seen lagging behind the others, but nevertheless uttering hoarse cries of encouragement from a position thirty or forty yards behind the ball. This is the captain. It is a safe bet to say that the standard of captaincy in the average club is as low as the standard of handling, which is to say a great deal.

Everyone recognises a good captain. His team wins. As long as a side keeps on being victorious the man nominally at their head will be considered a fine skipper.

It is not so easy to spot a bad captain. One infallible way is to listen what he shouts during a game. A good captain will either say something specific like 'Put it into touch' or will shut up. The bad captain delights in meaningless exhortations such as 'You're not getting stuck into them' or 'For heavens sake *do* something, forwards!'

For some reason captains of this sort loathe any move that varies even a fraction from the conventional. An attempt to make a deceptive 25-drop out merely brings forth a snarl and a shout of 'Cut out the fancy stuff.' The only way to gain approval is to put your head down and charge the opposition at their thickest point, when, after the carnage has settled with a gain of about six inches, the skipper will shout that that was great, that was the sort of stuff we want, not this fancy juggling (with fierce look at his harmless stand-off).

Such skippers have a wonderful knack of getting on the wrong side of the referee. They achieve this by snorting heavily at every decision against their side, muttering 'Oh God' and glaring at the offending official. The only effect this has is to increase the number of decisions against the team and if the referee has any sense he makes a mental note to warn all the other referees as well.

Another of their charming habits is to upset the biggest and toughest forward on the other side, usually shouting (from a safe distance) 'Cut that out you dirty bastard.' Then they keep well out of his way, leaving some innocent player to suffer the retribution.

If any member of their own team complains about anything they tell him to shut up. But if they feel injustice has been meted out to themselves, they demand complete support from all other fourteen men.

I shall not easily forget playing for a side whose skipper was ordered off the field (and quite rightly, too). He immediately turned to the rest of the team and demanded that they marched off in support of him. Fortunately we had enough sense to refuse, whereupon he announced that the whole side would be dropped next week for failing to obey captain's orders, and only the fact that he himself was expelled from the club on Monday evening stopped him carrying out this threat.

Perhaps, though, men like that are preferable to the bundle-of-energy type, the men who are determined to Transform the First Team. Such players rarely have any tactical knowledge, but believe that physical fitness conquers everything. The ball is never seen at training sessions, which consist of long cross-country runs, probably uphill and carrying sandbags.

The side is plagued by a host of injuries caused in training, and the constant cross-country running reduces everyone's match speed to a steady jog-trot. However, the team do have the satisfaction of knowing that if they can ever get within reach of their less fit, but more skilled, opponents they will pulverise them.

Captains like this often have high-sounding theories about physical fitness. They know a little elementary biology and take pleasure in telling players that the slope of their shoulders affects the leverage in the scrum, or that their bowels are too long, or some such gibberish. As a cure for bad passing they recommend sexual abstinence not only during a game, but before it, after it, and even when you've given up rugby. I knew one who issued a diet sheet for the First XV, and who would strike sandwiches from player's hands with a cry of 'Too much starch.'

Then there's the Whiz Kid. He does it all by exhortation and propaganda. Like the West London captain who stuck posters all over the clubhouse, urging everyone to greater efforts with slogans like :

IT ALL DEPENDS ON YOU

or

TACKLE! TACKLE! TACKLE!

He even wrote to every member of the team before a big game, urging them to maximum efficiency on the Saturday, but the letters didn't usually arrive until the Monday, when they had already lost heavily.

This captain was a great one for speeches, and he never lost an opportunity of addressing a team before a game. Unfortunately, his speech usually had the opposite effect to that intended.

'Listen lads,' he would shout, leaping on to a bench. 'This is a game we've simply got to win. We've got a few old scores to pay off against this lot. Remember what they did to Charlie Evans last season? Broke his leg in three places. And gave old Mike Fynn fourteen stitches in his head.

'Then there was poor Freddy Perch. Got five teeth knocked out in the return match. And Jack Smith was kicked unconscious. Are we taking this lying down?' At this point several weaker members of the side would turn pale and look around for a way of escape.

'Luckily,' the captain would remorselessly grind on, 'they've got the same team out as last year. Which means you've all got a chance to take revenge. In particular you want to watch that big front-row forward with the shaven head. Whatever happens, don't be frightened of him. He may weigh seventeen stone, but the bigger they are, the harder they fall . . .'

Having reduced his side to quivering apprehension, he would then lead them on to the field crying, 'O.K. lads, let's go, let's get stuck into them right away.'

The club newsletter provided him with a splendid platform and the captain's notes filled it page by page to the exclusion of more interesting material. At the annual dinner he used to ramble on for half-an-hour so the chief guest (who had probably driven 100 miles to be present) had to cut his speech to three minutes; at the annual meeting he went on for ever, unless physically restrained from talking. There was nothing to be done about him, he could talk his way into into almost everything, except victory.

Yet one must sympathise with a captain. It is a lonely task, made all the more difficult by the fact that sudden promotion can mean the end of old friendships. It's no use pretending people feel the same about their old pal when he drops them from the side. Nor when he rebukes them for using what used to be his favourite tactic, like deliberately collapsing the scrum to waste time.

The secret of successful leadership is a continual pose, the constant pretence of emotions you don't really feel, such as feigning anger that you're only two points up, when actually you're astonished not to be losing by twenty. For this reason, mournful men make the best leaders – they don't have to pretend. One of the most successful captains I met was a whining pessimist named Dismal Desmond, who never had a good word for anybody.

'Don't get over-confident' he used to groan, as the full-back banged over the fiftieth point. A winger who scored in the corner after running seventy yards would be told he ought to have touched down between the posts. Once he got the score wrong, thought a conversion had been dis-allowed and came off the field abusing us for losing.

'The worst performance I've ever seen,' he grumbled.

'Fancy losing to that lot. There'll be some changes in this team I can tell you.'

Even when someone explained that we had in fact *won* it made no difference.

'You needn't think that alters things' he snarled. 'We're having too many of these paper victories. There's more to winning than just scoring more points than the other side.'

But the most remarkable captain I served under was Basher Baker, an army sergeant who captained a training depot side in the war.

As far as Basher was concerned, a game of rugby was just another parade. He frequently stopped younger opponents by the sheer power of his voice, bellowing at some thrusting 18-year-old winger 'DROP THAT BALL! Yes, you there, it's you I'm talking to,' and such was the power of his personality that they invariably succumbed and probably stood to attention as well.

Basher had no hesitation in regarding bad play as a military crime and constant offenders found their rugby record mixed up with their military progress.

In this he was supported by the Major, and many a player, finding himself on a charge for not saluting properly, would be surprised to hear the C.O. say, 'Now then, I hear from Sergeant Baker that you've been behaving badly recently. He says you've been a very slack soldier, dropping passes and failing to fall on the ball when ordered to do so. This is a serious offence . . .'

Often whole squads of rugby players could be seen undergoing punishment, doubling round the square or swilling out latrines, especially after a heavy defeat.

To say we were terrified of Basher would be an understatement, but we had a mighty respect for him. I don't think he could exist today, not merely because the Army's changed but because the position of captain is being gradually eroded by the appointment of coaches. I don't know that that is such a bad thing. One can imagine a player of 2000 AD saying, 'But surely you don't mean that in the old days they had someone leading the team who didn't know anything about the game?' And one will reply, 'I'm sorry son, but only too frequently we did.'

D is for . . .

Dinner

Human beings have an incredible capacity for self-torture on social occasions, otherwise the amateur dramatic movement would have collapsed years ago. Rugby clubs are far from immune to this little failing, and are much prone to a form of self-induced suffering called the Annual Dinner.

The vilest form that this takes is the Prestige Dinner or Posh Nosh, an event much-beloved of London clubs. This is held in the West End, adding ten bob in fares to the four pounds members will be paying for their tickets, a good deal of which goes towards subsidising a swollen guest list, most of whom never wanted to come in the first place.

The menu is moderately extensive, but the portions would just about satisfy a starving gnat. The wine list looks like a builder's quotation for repairing Buckingham Palace. All wine arrives at the table lukewarm, irrespective of colour. So does the food. It will be served by swarthy little men who do not speak a word of English and who usually bring the wrong bottle.

Beer may also be served at ten shillings for each short pint of lukewarm foam. Change (if any) will arrive on a plate with a strong implication that it should be returned to the man who dispensed the foam.

Drinks after the meal are, with fiendish timing, served in the middle of a speech. The amount of noise and disturbance caused by this, and the desperate attempts of thirsty guests to order more, is increased by the waiter's habit of taking a five-pound note and vanishing with the change. At one dinner, near Piccadilly Circus, I gave the waiter a fiver for a two-pound bottle of wine and he promptly disappeared, not only from the restaurant, but apparently from the district, since no further trace of him could be discovered although we had six people searching every back alley for miles around.

Speaking at such functions is an ordeal. One is introduced by a bellowing idiot in a red coat calling himself the toastmaster, and the opening remark is probably drowned by an ear-splitting screech from the microphone. Subsequent remarks are made with the white-gloved hand of the insane toastmaster moving the microphone up and down in front of your face. Meanwhile, out front as it were, a riot appears to be going on as guests argue with waiters bringing the wrong drinks and disappearing with the change.

But eventually the proceedings drag to their conclusion and those guests who have not missed the last train can carry on drinking glasses of foam or whisky at prices which seem to increase as the hour gets later. This period gives senior members of the club a chance to bemoan the fact that younger players won't come to functions of this sort.

And as the last guest (usually a vice-president who has been sick over his evening suit) is helped into the lift, all is silence except for the sound of the staff counting money, a process that will probably take them all night.

Probably the most common dinner, however, is the Suburban Gin Palace Feast. This has the advantage that the price is more reasonable than in the West End, and the robbery less violent. Among the disadvantages are the fact that platoons of stout, middle-aged waitresses hover round the room during the early speeches, imposing a rigid censorship. Service of drinks after the meal ceases entirely, and the food is variable, and often made more unpalatable by the waitress's habit of thrusting her armpit into your face while serving it.

It's funny, but dinners of this sort seem to have a peculiar effect on visiting speakers. Having travelled out into the backwoods as it were, they become obsessed with the idea that it is their duty to educate these peasants. As the peasants don't feel like being educated, at least, not at the annual dinner, the speech turns into a sort of slanging match between the speaker and the club members.

Veins stand out on the speaker's forehead and he starts off in a manner that would make a Pharisee turn green with envy. 'Gentlemen,' he thunders, 'I would like to begin by saying that one of the things that distinguishes a rugger man from another is that he has a code. Tonight the behaviour of some of you has not conformed to that code.' (a piece of cucumber flies past his ear) 'I do not approve of trying to interfere with waitresses while they are serving soup for a start. Neither could I approve of the remarks of the previous speaker when he made irresponsible criticism of the amount of money the Rugby Union spends on banquets.

'Gentlemen . . . gentlemen . . . would you shut up at the back there . . . gentlemen . . . as I was saying earlier to your splendid President Mr Carpenter (cries of 'His name's Wright') . . . as I was saying to Mr Knight . . . we have to return to the old standards. Did someone ask what standards? I would say the old standards did not include throwing a piece of cucumber at the chief speaker !'

And so the battle continues for some ten minutes until the speaker gives up his educational efforts and sits down to scattered applause and a few boos from the far corner, while brushing the odd piece of cucumber from his coat.

Apart from speeches like the above (which are sometimes delivered by the nicest people), another hazard of the Gin Palace Dinner is the professional comedian who may be employed to entertain. Fortunately, they usually have to give up their act halfway through when the noise is so great that no one can hear a word, or indeed wants to.

The Club Supper is more informal and usually held in the pavilion. The food is not much worse than in the previous two examples, and the supply of drink a good deal better and cheaper, although the finer table wines may be lacking, and if served at all, will contain a generous percentage of cork and cigarette ash.

A target for bread rolls and sugar cubes

The object of any speaker at these functions is simply to provide a target for bread-rolls and sugar cubes, so that all he is expected to do is to stand up, remain vertical for three or four minutes, and sit down without losing his temper. If during that period he can recite every obscene word in the English language, so much the better. He will, in any case, probably find someone has stolen his speech notes if he left them on the table. Although once someone *burned* mine and had the cheek to return the ashes in a saucer with a note, 'Your speech was hot stuff.'

Occasionally, a professional stripper appears after the coffee. This eagerly-awaited and much whispered-about entertainment is normally an embarrassment, as the lady in question turns out to look rather like the captain's mother. Her performance is not improved by people pretending to be sick at her most tantalising movements, or trying to throw sugar lumps at her navel.

Unhappy though the above examples may be, they pale

B

before the dreaded Dinner-Dance, now becoming more and more popular.

The whole trouble with a dinner-dance is that owing to the presence of women it is not a dinner, and owing to the presence of rugby players, it is not a dance. The result is an evening unrelieved even by dirty jokes or snide references to the first-team threequarters. The main interest comes later when domestic squabbles break out between wives and husbands, and one realises why some players are always quite keen to come out training.

To make things worse, the seeds are sown of future infidelities. All too often, the result of holding a rugby club dinner-dance is that next season two legs of an eternal triangle will be found packing together in the second-row, with subsequent dire results on the playing record.

You have been warned.

E is for . . .

Excuses

Rugby is the game of excuses. This is not surprising when one considers what is required of the average player. The game has been designed, if played properly, to require immense stores of courage, physical endurance, instant decision even when threatened with three raging forwards, alertness, speed, self-control, the ability to assess what 29 other men on the field are doing in a split second and act accordingly, and the learning of some 400 paragraphs of laws (which are constantly being altered to make the game faster).

And as if all that were not enough, a player is supposed to *smile* when hurled into the stand, grin when injured, shake hands with the man who kicked him, cheer him off the field, buy him beer afterwards, and finally pay a substantial match fee for the privilege.

No wonder then that mere ordinary mortals are continually having to make excuses for their conduct on or off the field. These range from almost genuine ones such as, 'It was your fault' to classics of invention like, 'Just as he passed to me I remembered I had left the bath water running at home . . .'

The perfect rugby excuse should be as far away from the truth as possible. Rugby players, like other mortals, are given to fantasies, and if asked why you shirked a tackle, it is absolutely no use saying 'Because I am a coward, skipper.' True this may be, but it will only earn abuse.

Whereas an outrageous lie, something like, 'My rupture was troubling me' or 'The leg which I broke saving those children from a runaway horse gave way again' will be accepted with only a grunt, and an exhortation to do better next time. Note that in the examples given, the blame is cunningly transferred to the captain, with the inference that he has abused a sick man.

A great deal of ingenuity is needed in making a good excuse, however. It is absolutely no use at all simply to blurt forth the first untruth that comes into the head. A player who concedes a penalty for offside is wasting his time if he says, 'It wasn't my fault. I was yards on. The ref's blind.'

What is needed is something much more subtle, on the lines of 'Sorry lads, but we all know this ref has hated me ever since I proved him wrong at Sidcup . . .'

The ingenuity of this excuse is that it brings the skipper and the rest of the team on the side of the offender, so that after the match the team and the captain can use the same excuse for defeat, saying, 'We never had a hope. Charlie told us the referee has always had a down on us since he messed up that game at Sidcup last year . . .'

Thus the chain of fantasy goes on and on, until a year or two later some perfectly innocent and competent referee finds himself officiating at Sidcup and being greeted with snarls and hoots of derision for some reason he cannot understand.

Here then, are some suggested excuses to meet given situations :

On dropping a pass
    'These damn contact lenses !'
    'You may call it a pass but it looked like a cunning dummy to me . . .'
    'Didn't you hear me call "Scissors" ?'

On giving a bad pass
    'Poor Fred's eyes aren't what they used to be.'
    'Poor Fred's hands aren't what they used to be.'
    'Poor Fred isn't what he used to be.'

On refusing to fall on the ball
    'I hate negative rugby. We want to open up the game, not close it down.'

On failing to win the strike in a set scrum

'I deliberately let them have the ball as a tactical move.'

'Fred put the ball at their feet. His eyes aren't what they used to be.'

On failing to score

'I injured my knee training last week. I always said strenuous training does more harm than good.'

On failing to turn up for training

'I injured my knee playing last week.'

'Standing for an hour in a tube train is harder exercise than running five miles.'

'All this training is making us stale.'

On being intimidated

'I *did* stand up to him. I told him to "—— off" under my breath.'

On shirking a tackle

'I had *my* man covered. Maybe he didn't have the ball, but so what? Go for your own man is the golden rule. Fred should have got him.'

On failing to score

'OK, OK, so maybe I should have been able to run ten yards and touch down. Didn't you realise I was still blind in one eye after that match-saving tackle ten minutes before? Think yourself lucky I didn't leave the field.'

On everything

'The referee was a clot.'

'Look, I hate to keep mentioning this but you force me to remind you that I have a steel plate in my hip.'

CAPTAIN'S EXCUSES

On losing 48-nil
'It's that stupid *fixture* secretary. He ought to have known their winger once had a Scottish cap.'

On turning out with twelve men
'It's that stupid *team* secretary,' etc., etc.

On arriving half-an-hour after kick-off
'It's that stupid *secretary* of ours.'

On losing when he should have won easily
'No one will ever beat them as long as they have that touch-judge.'
'I would rather play clean and lose, than play dirty like them and win.'

REFEREE'S EXCUSES

On failing to award a perfectly good try
'Someone was standing in my way.'
'These contact lenses!'
'Try? What try?'

On disallowing a good mark
'My deaf aid isn't working very well.'

On playing forty-nine minutes in the second half
'The pavilion clock is wrong.'
'Why is there no pavilion clock?'

On not sending a player off for biting
'The skin wasn't actually broken, you know.'

On sending off the wrong man
　　'Well it may not have been him that time, but he deserved to go anyway. He's continually offended Law 14.'

For failing to warn a dirty player
　　'I looked at him severely.'

F is for . . .

Fiona

Fiona telephones:

'Hullo, hullo ... is that you, Penelope? Yes it's *me*, Fiona. Yes, I *know* it's strange to ring someone up on your honeymoon night, but I've just got to tell you.... Rodney can't do it! What's that? No, darling, he can do *that* – well, just, at any rate – but he can't come to the sevens with you and Jonathan next week. Why not? Darling, he's in gaol. Yes, dear, that place where they put your Daddy after he smashed up the Jag ... no, I'm not trying to drag up old wounds ... Yes Darling, it must have been positively grotty in Pentonville ... well you see, it was all the result of the wedding. Yes, I know you couldn't be there. Yes, dear, we did thank you for the cake-dish. And everyone else who gave cakedishes. It was all Daddy's fault really. He started drinking at dawn. I know he did because he got up early to make the tea and when I came down an hour later he hadn't even put the kettle on – he was just sitting by the radiator with a bottle of champagne. I asked him what he was doing and he said it was the happiest day of his life. No, dear, it was *not* a nice thing to say. He didn't mean it as a compliment. Well, honestly, by the time he came to take me to the church he was in a terrible state. He couldn't find his top hat anywhere and we had to go without it. Then he insisted on opening the car windows and shouting at people in the street. I don't know what the driver thought, but we got to what Daddy insisted on calling the "sacred edifice" all right, and Mummy and I got him inside by holding each arm, and I sort of led him up the aisle. And then we went through the ceremony and Rodney looked absolutely monumental in his morning-suit and it all went like a bomb until they came to that bit "with my body I thee worship" at which Daddy

burst out into peals of drunken laughter and Mummy had to
put her hand over his mouth to shut him up. The vicar
looked outraged, especially as he hates Daddy ever since he
took change for ten bob from the collecting-plate. Then he
loudly asked if there was any just cause or impediment and
so forth, and of course there was complete silence, and in
the middle of it all a Welsh voice muttered quite distinctly
"I should think there was" and I realised that awful creature
Taffy Owen had got into church. He was sitting with the
rest of the fourth XV at the back. Anyway, to cut a long
story short, we got through it all (although I didn't like the
way Rodney hesitated on "I do") and we marched out down
the aisle and when we got outside there were the players
with an arch of corner flags. It was wonderful. And then to
my horror as we were marching under this arch I saw
Taffy holding one of the flags and as we passed he said
quite distinctly, "I've had her. And I didn't enjoy it."
Honestly, I nearly *died*. And Rodney must have heard,
because he got all sort of tensed up and he's always been
jealous of Taffy but that's old history now. Well, anyway, off
we went to the reception and Daddy was *beastly*, he kept slap-
ping Rodney on the back and shouting, "Better you than me,
old son," and pouring brandy into his champagne, and then
he went over and actually shook Taffy by the hand, although
he hadn't even been invited. I thought I was going to *howl*.
Well, eventually we got to the speeches, and it was obvious
by then that Rodney had been affected by Daddy's champagne and brandy because instead of just saying a few words
he went on and on and on. And then he started to become
absolutely revolting and began making alleged humorous remarks like, "As a good forward I shall certainly push hard
tonight," and then he told the most obscene story I have ever
heard in all my life and Mummy's relatives' faces were going
blacker and blacker and I just sat there *frozen* with horror.
I was sure Uncle George was going to make a scene. Mercifully Rodney forgot the end of his story and Tubby Chap-

man, the best man, leapt up and thanked him and said he might be a joke as a full-back but he was sure he would find touch tonight, and they all howled with mirth and Daddy fell off his chair. Eventually Mummy and I had literally to drag Rodney away so we could change, and we were going to be driven in Tubby's car only when we got outside, it had been jacked up and all four wheels removed. So we went in Daddy's car (thank heavens Daddy refused to drive and Tubby did instead) and came back in Rodney's to say goodbye. Well, believe it or not it took another hour and a half to get Rodney away and a lot of it was Daddy's fault, he kept getting them together in a scrum and heeling someone's top hat. Eh? No, I don't know whose hat it was... Taffy's, I hope... but eventually we got away and drove off to the secret honeymoon hotel... no, dear, no-where very exciting, Henley-on-Thames if you must know. Rodney had originally booked us in at Maidenhead but I made him change it. Well, there *is* a limit... Anyway, on the way, the most cataclysmic event occurred. A policeman stopped us on the Motorway and asked Rodney if he was aware that he had *a stair-carpet trailing from the back of the car*. They must have tied it on while we were waving goodbye. Well, to cut a long story short, the policeman got a sniff of Rodney's breath (not that that was difficult, you could have smelt the brandy five hundred yards away) and asked him to breathe into a bag and Rodney hiccupped and said he had a right to trail a stair-carpet if he wanted, and the policeman said, "Not when it's got Star and Garter Hotel printed all over it,' and then Rodney was rude to the police-man and the next thing I remember was sitting in the police station while they locked Rodney in some dungeon or other, and told me he'd come before the magistrate in the morning. So here's little Fionakins sitting in the bridal suite at Henley-on-Thames on her ownsome and all her friends imagining her revelling in an orgy of positive lust. No, dear, I don't intend to come back to London tonight. Can you imagine what Daddy would say if his own daughter rang the front doorbell on her honeymoon night? Besides, I've got to attend the trial or what ever they call it, tomorrow . . . and to think I voted for the return of flogging at the Young Conservatives . . .'

G is for . . .

Grounds

In the same way as no ship can be *really* ugly to the sea-lover, so no rugby ground, however vile, can be utterly detestable to the rugby enthusiast. The very fact that the familiar posts are there is enough to hallow it. Even so, the most fanatical exponent of the game must sometimes wince at the places where rugby is played.

The grounds of first-class clubs do at least have such amenities as a stand and pavilion to soften any harshness; for the others there may be nothing to break the bleak monotony of the scenery except an odd slag heap or electricity pylon. Even the pavilion (if any) may be miles away.

The greatest ground of all, Twickenham, presents two faces. Packed for an international it is a wonderful place, both for watching and for walking round. But occupied by only a few hundred spectators for a Quins' or Services' game, it can be the most dismal spot on earth, every solitary shout echoing through the vast, deserted caverns of the stands.

It's when the stands are full that Twickenham comes into its own. In some respects it's like Lord's, the headquarters of its own game and the great Mecca of enthusiasts the world over. But Lord's has only one Tavern as the meeting-place of the *cognoscenti* (and they've wrecked that by rebuilding it and replacing it with an ordinary bar). At Twickenham there's more than half-a-dozen places, each with its regular patrons, where the fans gather to drink and talk in conditions of unutterable discomfort.

At Twickenham the tradition is to keep moving before and after the match, thanks to the ample promenading space around the stands. If you walk round long enough you'll meet people you haven't seen for years. There's always the odd feeling that although 70,000 people are there, everyone really knows everyone else and it's just a parish outing for the Rugby fraternity with incidental entertainment kindly supplied by 30 international players.

This has its disadvantages. Elderly bores approach and fixing one with a watery eye insist you played against Old Millhillians' third team in 1956. And if one meets old friends, old enemies are there as well. I once came face to face with a man I had last seen being carried off the field, shouting that he would get me if it took him the rest of his life (he wrongly suspected me of breaking his ankle, but it was the full-back who had tripped him). We stared at each other in embarrassment for a moment and then slunk away in opposite directions, only to meet again the other side of the ground (which is typical of Twickenham).

It was at Twickenham, ten minutes before the end of a Varsity match, that a man once walked into the deserted West Bar, where the servers were having a last smoke before the big rush, and ordered 118 pints of beer. What's more he got them, along with sundry light ales and a few Scotches. Somehow one can't see that happening anywhere else. The man who gave the gigantic order was an official of the B.M.R.F.C., an interesting rugby club that has never lost a match, largely because it never plays any. The B.M. (Bloody Men) exists chiefly for the purpose of watching big rugby matches with the maximum of lubrication.

Their great moment came when their coach was mistaken for that of the R.A.F. Band, and police escorted it into the ground. The secretary of the Rugby Union came out to greet the band, and on being confronted with several familiar faces and a strong smell of beer as he opened the coach door, commented bitterly, 'If I'd known it was you lot, I wouldn't have bothered.'

Another interesting Twickenham tradition is the car-park picnic. Probably no nation but the English would enjoy a meal of cold chicken and whisky in air made poisonous by the stench of 10,000 exhausts, not to mention two or three degrees of frost and a hint of fog.

But one of the main things that distinguishes Twickenham from other great sporting centres is the way people stay on after the match. At White City, or Wembley or the Oval they can't get away quick enough. At Twickenham they're still around hours after the game has finished.

They shut the bars earlier these days after they once had to call the fire brigade to the West Bar, where they were greeted by the chant of, 'We call on the firemen to sing us a song . . .' But even so, there's still hundreds of people around when darkness falls, just strolling around, or indulging in such innocent pastimes as piling up beer cans and knocking them down again. Perhaps that is the finest tribute Twickenham could have – people don't hurry to get away from it.

Which is more than can be said of some other rugby grounds. Harlequins, for instance, not only have the dubious privilege of playing in an empty Twickenham, but play their other home games in the cold remoteness of the Stoop Ground, where a running track makes sure spectators don't get too close. Mercifully, the bar is one of the cosiest in London.

Wasps probably give spectators a warmer welcome than any other club. They actually smile and wave your car inside. At Richmond Athletic ground the reverse holds good, and visiting teams have been refused admittance because they forgot their passes. Some referees are said to have been reduced to *paying* to get in and do their job.

Outside London, it would be difficult to beat Northampton, which like Twickenham has a strong tradition of spectators staying after the game. Until they built the new pavilion, Northampton boasted an amenity surely unique in any first-class game, a Players' Bar under the stand run by the players for the benefit of the spectators (and the players). Here, payment of a nominal membership fee entitled you to be served by a choice of anything up to three internationals.

As a Leicester-born man I naturally have a great deal of affection for the Leicester ground. This is partly because it was there that I played the only first-class game of rugby in

my life, for a Combined Leicester XV against the Tigers
themselves (Leicester's first home game after the end of World
War Two). I quite seriously thought of having my boots
preserved in surgical spirit as a souvenir, but being rather
young at the time I couldn't afford a new pair. There is a
fascinating air of decaying grandeur about Welford Road,
with its big stands, a reminder that internationals were played
there until 1923. Still, the Tigers manage to fill it once a
year when they play the Barbarians. Another Leicester
ground remembered with affection by thousands is Victoria
Park, home of the redoubtable Leicester Thursday, one of a
few open mid-week clubs left. I always consider it more
of a privilege to have played for Thursday than for any
other club. They were the sort of team who would tell an
international three-quarter that he'd have to play in the
forwards to make room for Charlie because Charlie worked
in a shop and this was the only game he got in the week.
Despite this, Victoria Park has probably seen more international rugby players than any other public park in the
country, thanks to Thursday's habit of playing Leicester members midweek. We used to change in the disused stables
behind the Old Horse Hotel and charge across London
Road carrying the posts like spears. A tram route ran by the
park and latecomers were liable to leap from the tram as
it ran by the touchline and join in the game without delay.

Changing in an old bus by the side of a meadow that formed
the old Notts Tigers pitch is another vivid memory; and
so are the howling wastes of Wanstead Flats, East London,
with their gaslit changing rooms and gaping holes in the floor-
boards, although they've probably got new accommodation
now. In London, however, my favourite ground was Horsen-
den Hill, Ealing, because it was there I played my declining
years of rugby until eventually I convinced myself I'd have
a heart attack if I went on any longer. I also managed to
convince the rest of the team that they had the symptoms,
too. They used to beg me to stop telling them how dangerous

it was if you felt a singing in the ears. We reached such a state of nerves, that frequently a player would be seen standing stock still in the middle of the field anxiously feeling his pulse, and nobody thought it was unusual, except the opposition.

We used to change in a pub and our sole washing facilities were two ordinary household baths for both teams. They didn't have running water and we used to carry them into the landlord's garage before the game and fill them from buckets afterwards. There isn't much room for 30 people in two baths, as might be imagined, and it usually took up to two hours before the last player staggered forth. Towards the end, the water, apart from being stone-cold, became a sort of muddy porridge, and those who washed last merely turned a sort of khaki colour all over. Some of the hardier spirits used to hose each other down from the cold tap and once a couple of maniacs rolled naked in the car-park snow.

Perhaps it is not surprising that the most common reason for dropping out of the side was rheumatism.

H is for . . .

Handling

Considering that rugby is supposed to be a handling game, it is astonishing the number of players, at all levels, who are quite unable either to give or take a pass. It's only comparitively recently, that anyone has ever worried about this, ever since the French started beating us by *cheating*, i.e. using forwards to run with the ball.

Until 1950 most forwards weren't even supposed to know how to pass, and if they had to transfer the ball, they weren't expected to use the normal threequarter's pass, but a special one of their own, in which the arms were only used from the elbows. This was based on the theory that no respectable English forward would ever want to pass more than three feet, and if he did he should be damned well ashamed of himself. Forwards who threw long passes were equated with players who left the clubhouse early on Saturday nights to meet women.

I talk about this attitude to handling as if it was something in the past but there are still plenty of clubs where it holds good; where the forwards solemnly shuffle down the field at training, painfully handing the ball to each other from close-range, while the backs train separately, as if they were going to play some totally different game.

Why the whole basis of rugby should be its most neglected aspect I don't know. Perhaps because of the English amateur tradition, that it's not good form to be too proficient at anything. Chaps who dance along the touchline balancing the ball on the end of their index finger have an unpleasant whiff of professionalism about them. Players who juggle desperately with the simplest of passes before knocking the ball forward three yards, couldn't possibly be anything but amateur.

The schools must share some of the blame for handling

An unpleasant whiff of professionalism

standards. Frequently hours are wasted teaching boys a series of insane regulations such as passing off the correct foot, swerving the body and keeping the arms rigid (although they often forget the most important thing of all, which is to watch the man you're passing to). All this produces a peculiar English form of pass, The Public School Swoosh, in which the passer is concentrating so much on the perfect action that he runs straight into an opponent while trying to remember not to bend his arms.

Other interesting results of this type of pass are that the passer falls over while swerving smartly to one side, and that he telegraphs his intentions all over the field.

The swoosh is mercifully seen much less frequently these days, thanks to improved coaching. But there are many other types of pass which merit attention, some accidental rather than deliberate.

Probably the most frequently-used pass in rugby is the Helicopter. This is seen at its most typical when a fourth team forward receives the ball ten yards from his opponents' line, with no one to beat. Does he stick his head down grimly, and with a snort of defiance head for the line? Or does he dance and swerve his way there, leaving would-be tacklers clutching the empty air?

No, he doesn't. What he does do is emit a ghastly shout of horror, stare wildly about him, and then *throw the ball vertically into the air*. It's no use saying that is exaggerated, if anything it's an understatement. It happens nearly every time.

Various theories may be put forward to account for this astonishing behaviour. It is not necessarily cowardice. The player is not afraid of any opponent, *he is afraid of the ball*.

This is partly caused by intensive conditioning. Perhaps the unhappy player remembers when he was rebuked for running with the ball, and told a forward's job was to put his head down and shove. Or maybe years in the Extra B have sapped his self-confidence. After all, people aren't put in the fourth team because of their strength, sagacity, speed and scrummaging power. You're there because either you aren't fit for anything else, or else you have offended the club authorities in some way.

Most players realise this. Years of being ground down in the rubbish-bin of rugby football produces a sort of mental stupefaction. What more natural then, that a player on receiving the ball should instinctively think, 'Good God, this is an honour I can't face. It's all too much for me,' and sling the ball vertically in the air?

As an example of this, let me quote the case of an old Midland forward who, having made a Helicopter pass, begged not to be given the ball again. 'I never know what to do with the blasted thing, Alf,' he told the captain, and his request was accepted as reasonable and logical in that class of football.

I would say that the second most common type of pass is the White Feather, so-called because it is an act of sheer fright by a terrified player. Signs that it is approaching start long before it is made, since the man with the ball will be seen running sideways, or even backwards, never taking his eyes from the potential tacklers.

When some fifteen yards from the nearest opponent, the player (still staring straight ahead) will take the ball in one hand and hurl it backwards over his shoulder somewhere in the vague direction of his own full-back. Without waiting to see the results of this, he will then immediately fall over.

This pass is by no means restricted to the lower grades of rugby, and is even seen in first-class clubs who are playing stern opposition. Even internationals are guilty, but they usually manage to make it look like a cleverly-planned tactical move gone wrong, rather than an act of self-preservation. Strangely enough, the craven passer often fails to save his own skin, and is frequently injured by being knocked over while nowhere near the ball.

The Gay Cavalier pass has been responsible for more lost games than any other factor in rugby football. Its maker is inevitably a centre threequarter, usually blond, who shatters the defence with a stunning break, flees for the line with his hair streaming behind him like a great mane, carefully draws the full-back and then hurls the ball with unerring accuracy two feet above the head of the unmarked winger, usually with such force that it goes deep into the crowd.

On one occasion in London, I actually saw a centre-threequarter pass direct into a No. 93 bus which was coming along an adjacent road. I may say that the conductor's return was considerably more accurate than the original pass.

One of the interesting psychological aspects of the Gay Cavalier is that the passer has no sense of guilt whatever, and walks back to the centre of the pitch, tossing his head and smiling, stopping only to say to the aggrieved winger, 'Bad luck old chap, *but we all miss them now and then.*'

If this should happen, resist any temptation to throw the ball at his face as he will have absolutely no idea that he has done anything wrong.

Various positions on the field often have their own types of pass.

Scrum-halves are prone to The Whirlitzer, the inevitable result of trying to pretend that you really do have a long pass, it just needs time to get there. The passer usually makes a tremendous fuss about delivering the ball, arching his back and flinging himself into puddles with great abandon.

The ball is sent at an angle of 45 degrees upwards and hangs agonisingly at the top of its parabola before descending somewhere near the unfortunate stand-off, who is by now shaking hands with a particularly large wing-forward on the other side.

A variation of this is the Casualty Ward, where the scrum-half runs with his head down in a tiny ineffectual semi-circle, waits until the stand-off is surrounded and then squirts the ball to him from under his armpit.

Front-row forwards are prone to a particular pass of their own, The Presentation. Upon deciding to pass, a spasm crosses the face of the player, who then takes the ball carefully in both hands, rotates the upper half of his body carefully, and solemnly hands the ball, like a silver cup, to someone two feet away. For some reason which I can never fathom, he always finds it necessary to stop running to do this.

Usually the best passing in a team will be by the full-back. Getting rid of the ball for him is often the only way of avoiding a hideous death or serious injury. Most full-backs are capable of passing under incredible difficulties, using only the power of one finger, or even their teeth.

Finally there's a pass which doesn't exist – the Press Box Pass. The Press Box Pass exists only in the minds of sports reporters (including myself) and is usually described thus : 'England lost a great chance of going ahead when Smith broke through in the centre, only to ignore Robinson on his right and die with the ball near the line.'

The truth is, of course, that although Robinson was indeed on the right, he was thirty yards away, there was a high wind blowing, and three opponents were in the way of any pass. More important still, Smith was far too busy with his own problems, the chief of which was that he never thought he would break through, and having done so he hadn't the faintest idea what to do next. Not to mention the fact that he knew unless he did something spectacular this was his last appearance for England.

A New Zealander once told me a novel passing theory. He said his team used to work on the principle that the *receiver* is always to blame for a pass going astray, on the theory that everyone should be alert to take the ball at all times.

But alas, one can't see the English temperament accepting a rule like that. Any man who said, 'I'm sorry I dropped your pass, old chap. Even though it hit my foot, I still ought to have gathered it,' would be regarded as perpetrating some obscure insult.

No, far better stick to the good old English tradition, that it doesn't matter whether a pass is accurate as long as you give it in the approved manner.

H is also for . . .

Half-time

A cynic once suggested that the reason rugby players don't leave the field at half-time is because most of them wouldn't come back. It is, of course, forbidden without the referee's permission. Because of this, the rugby half-time, even at international level presents an odd contrast with that of the League soccer clubs. While the rugby players stand around steaming in the rain soccer men are resting in the changing-room and probably having egg-nog, oxygen and massage as well. They are also getting a thorough going-over from the manager whereas at least the rugby player is safely out of reach of the selection committee or the aggrieved club chairman.

A few players would prefer to do without half-time, as they say the rest makes them stiffen up but these people are maniacs who should be ignored. For the average player, half-time comes as a golden couple of minutes of pleasure in an afternoon of unrelieved physical torture, and there are several ways in which he can make the most of this wonderful respite.

First, when the whistle blows, do not give way to the temptation to fall face downwards on the ground, gasping for breath or groaning feebly. This creates a bad impression on the skipper and encourages the other side. Try to stay upright, if necessary by limping to the goal and holding on to one of the posts.

If in any distress, it is best to ask the referee's permission to leave the field, since standing around in three degrees of frost hardly improves one's physical condition. In fact it is best to do so whether in distress or not. I recall with great pleasure how myself and a little group of friends always used to go to the pavilion at half-time, ostensibly for a call of nature, but in reality to get into the boiler-room and sit around on the hot pipes. The trouble was we used to lose all sense of time, especially if we played cards, and they frequently had to send the full-back to fetch us back. Or else we would return to find the team lining up to face a conversion while the captain shook his fist at us.

But leaving the field has its dangers. If you've had a bad first half, go off via touch-in-goal. Don't let any committee members have the chance to get near you. Ignore anyone like the coach or chairman who beckons to you. If such officials should come on the field at half-time leave immediately in the opposite direction, despite any shouting or cries to return. Don't come back until it's safe to do so.

There is another danger in going to the pavilion. You might not have the strength to get back. I am not joking. I have seen an elderly player leave at half-time for a pavilion which was half a mile away at the other side of the playing-fields. To save time he ran all the way there. When play was due to re-start we looked for him and saw his grey-haired figure wheezing towards us 800 yards away.

Everyone started waving and shouting and he broke into a shambling sort of trot but after he'd gone another 50 yards he actually had to sit down on a park seat to have a rest.

The referee wouldn't wait any longer so we started the game. Every time there was a stoppage we looked towards the pavilion and discovered that the missing player was moving towards us a 100 yards at a time, stopping to sit down at every bench, where he would smile and wave feebly at us. He eventually arrived ten minutes after the kick-off and said by way of explanation, 'I made the mistake of smoking a fag after running half a mile. I shall have to give up running.'

Even worse was the case of a player who at the same ground actually picked up a girl on his way back from the pavilion. She was sitting on a seat with her dog and he bent down and patted the dog and then sat down beside her and started to chat her up. Of course, everyone was shrieking at him to come back, but he just waved at us and smiled, and carried on talking.

By the time we kicked-off he was holding her hand. He didn't return until we sent a deputation to drag him back, and then he spent most of the game waving to her from the scrums and blowing kisses in the line-outs.

Sometimes it is not possible to leave the field. The main disadvantage of this, apart from the physical discomfort, is that one has to listen to the captain's half-time chat. The chief theme of this is phony optimism about the side's prospects. I never knew a captain who would be really honest and say, 'Well, lads, they're much better than us, we obviously haven't a hope, so don't bust your guts this half, save a little energy for the club dance tonight.'

Instead, they go through the ghastly charade of pretending that it will all come right if everyone *tries* a bit harder (ignoring the fact that the opposition are really winning because they have carefully rehearsed their line-out drill). However, it is fatal to express disagreement with this load of codswallop. Nod occasionally and rub the knee as if an injury has been received (you may need the excuse later).

Finally, there is the referee, who during half-time normally stands alone, uneasily aware that both sides are looking at him and then spitting. It is not a happy time for him but he must not weaken. The time can be put to good advantage by working out little problems, such as how to deal with that big forward who keeps obstructing, without sending him off.

One temptation he must resist at all costs. The referee must never be seen to drag out the R.U. Handbook from his pocket and start looking up the laws. If you want to check what the penalty is for obstruction in in-goal, leave the field and do it secretly, preferably under your raincoat.

I is for . . .

Impediments

One of the most important things a rugby player can learn is a knowledge of the various impediments and hazards that are likely to affect him and his team before, during and after a match. I am not referring to playing obstacles, but to those unexpected incidents unconnected with the actual play, which add so much spice to the life of the rugby player, especially in the game's lower regions.

Animals, of course, are a perpetual source of interruption and there is no need to dwell on the nuisance caused by dogs, sheep and cows. I have, however, had the interesting experience of being forced to move to another pitch because a goat had chewed through one of the goalposts.

Lions have been known to interrupt games in Africa. At least, so I am told by an old friend, who assures me that he refereed a match in which he was astonished when suddenly both teams, and the scattering of spectators, fled from the field, leaving him standing there blowing his whistle.

Eventually, cries of 'Simba! Simba!' from the African players, most of whom were up trees by now, drew his attention to the animal, which showed every inclination to go to sleep by the goal-posts.

'I couldn't have that' said the referee, 'so I pointed at him and blew a long blast'. The surprised lion shambled away – probably the first and last lion ever to be sent off a rugby field.

Normally, however, it will be the human element which will be the cause of most hazards. The most common of human-inspired hazards is undoubtedly *Elderly Idiot Cycling Across Pitch*.

This danger exists primarily on public parks, although it can happen on enclosed grounds. It is most frequent when the playing-area is bordered by allotments in which case the

Employ him as a shield for running behind . . .

offender will wobble wildly across the pitch with two sacks of seed potatoes and a garden rake slung over his back.

Never attempt to interfere with these people as upon being approached they inevitably fall off their bicycles, and this means the rider will probably spear his foot with a garden fork, and then you will *never* get him off the pitch. In addition he will shout and rave at all and sundry, bellowing insults like, 'Yer didn't oughter be allowed on 'ere, yer young hooligans, I'll report the lot of yer' etc. etc.

The only suggestion I can make for coping with an elderly idiot cycling cross the pitch is to *use* him. Employ him as a shield for running behind and you will quickly find how difficult it is to tackle someone running behind a wobbling bicycle.

Banning of game by park-keeper is another frequent hazard. The ban may be imposed because you didn't pay last week, because you're on the wrong pitch, because it's getting dark, because the keeper alleges the pitch is unfit, or out of sheer cussedness.

The main point to remember is that nothing on earth will change a park-keeper's mind. They are a special breed of men, deaf to all reason and pleading (otherwise they wouldn't be park-keepers). Pointing out that the pitch is in perfect condition, offering money, threatening to complain, is worse than useless.

The only thing to do is ignore them completely. Play on as if nothing had happened, despite the fact that the wretched man is probably ringing a great bell at the side of the pitch. Eventually, he may walk on to the field of play and try to impound the ball, but it should not be too difficult to keep it away from him as park-keepers have a special type of walk, rather as if they were carrying a banner in a procession, which prevents their travelling at any speed.

Policemen rushing on to the field require different treatment. They will usually march on to complain about a parking offence, although in extreme cases I have known a policeman drive his motor-cycle across the pitch. Their normal channel of approach is via the touch-judge, although they utterly ignore his protestations, 'You can't go on there.'

Under no circumstances attempt to continue the game or they will get out their notebook and ask the full-back his name just as the other side are about to score.

Do not try to pretend that nobody knows anything about the car parked in the middle of the North Circular Road. The offender is somewhere around, desperately bluffing his way out of it. Make him confess and hand him over to justice without any mercy, adding sycophantic remarks like, 'You ought to be ashamed of yourself giving that nice policeman all that trouble.'

Believe me, once a copper is set on his pound of flesh, he's going to get it. Any effort to shield the offender will merely result in an examination of every car parked around the ground, and twenty summonses for such offences as having the rear number-plate obscured. The only person without a summons will probably be the chap who caused all the trouble in the first place.

N.B. Never say to a policeman, 'Would you like a game, officer?'

A mishap I have experienced more than once is *Sudden Mysterious Explosion of the Ball*. This usually has nothing to do with its being forcibly kicked – it just goes off for no reason, probably age.

The traditional rule is the best here – if the first team's ball explodes, they are entitled to borrow one from the next lowest side, and so on, down the scale until the fifth team stop playing (it is quite certain they won't have a spare ball).

A few seconds' consideration will show that this is a just and reasonable procedure, because the fifth team will be delighted at this opportunity to abandon the match and get into the bath before everybody else.

And finally, a hazard that often faces a player after the game, *Failure of Hot Water Boiler*.

If that happens, never wash in cold water. It gives you sores in winter weather. Simply leave the mud on like a plaster. It holds the warmth, and you will be surprised how comfortable you will feel for the rest of the evening. If you are married, however, try to bath before going to bed.

J is for . . .

Journalist

Many years ago the sports editor of a London newspaper sent me to report a Second Division soccer match. 'We want someone who will bring a really fresh mind to soccer,' he said, although he really meant, 'You're on your way out, chum.' Despite the fact that I hadn't seen a League soccer match for 20 years I obliged, and, aided by a friendly local reporter, managed to scramble through some sort of account of the game, after which I was invited to be the guest of the directors in the Board Room.

For a former third XV stand-off, the scene in the Board Room seemed a sportsman's paradise, that is if your idea of heaven is drinking endless quadruple whiskies, soaked up with delicious cucumber sandwiches. After half-an-hour, and four multiple scotches, I decided that I'd misjudged soccer all these years. If this was what they did every Saturday night then this was the game for me.

Full of goodwill I lurched up to the club chairman (who by now had turned purple and was breathing with difficulty) and said, 'This is the best party I've been to for years. I suppose you start the singing when the players come in?'

He looked at me as if I had said something unspeakable and replied frostily, 'We don't have *them* in here.'

This seems to me to sum up the difference between reporting rugby and most other games. There is no Us and Them in rugby, and a reporter won't get invited anywhere a player can't go, although he will be banned from going to places in which a player *can* go. In the great amateur game the reporter gets treated like everybody else, and I write as one who was invited by North Midlands to their team banquet and then handed a bill for my meal.

This also shows itself in the attitude of individual players,

Capable of showing a healthy contempt for the Press

who are capable of showing a healthy contempt for the Press. Attempts to interview a winger in the shower after the game and ask him how he felt when he dropped the vital pass are liable to be met with some remark like, 'How do you think I felt, you stupid bastard?' (although this may well appear in the paper as 'I was numb with dismay').

This difficulty of getting something coherent from a player is largely responsible for the continual annual appearance of the The Silent Genius of British Rugby. Every year, British rugby produces its silent wizard, The Man Who Thinks about the Game, but whose lips are sealed.

The reason is simply the difficulty of getting the wretched man to *talk*. Upon being asked, 'What do you think of the new laws?' he is quite likely to reply 'What new laws?' Efforts to worm out the philosophy behind his play meet with remarks such as, 'When I sees the ball I puts me head down and has a go, like.'

The only way of dealing with such a man is to ask leading questions ('You would agree, then, that rugby is a dynamic as opposed to a static tactical operation?') and take the stupified look of amazement on his face as assent. This enables the reporter to turn out a feature piece entitled THE SILENT EINSTEIN OF ENGLISH RUGBY in which the astonished player finds himself quoted as saying, 'Rugby boils down to a question of simple mathematics. A game like a sine curve. The important thing is to remember the power of X.'

But although players tend to be uncommunicative, club officials are embarrassingly ready to spill the beans. Once again, a different situation from other sports, where events that have split the club from top to bottom will officially be described as a slight difference of opinion between the manager and the board.

If a reporter sits long enough in a rugby club bar someone is sure to come up and ask naïvely if he heard about what happened in committee the other evening. 'I don't know if you ought to print this old chap, but Fred said he would never play for the first team again unless Bert resigned. Something to do with a woman.'

Alas, the truth is inevitably too strong to be told and the spectator is left wondering why for several weeks a certain London club never has its two internationals playing together, and why eventually, one leaves for another club.

The actual reporting of matches, too, is often done under severe physical handicaps. I have reported a county game where the Press-table consisted of six empty beer crates on end, until we drank a couple of dozen light ales and got another crate to sit on. Even where proper Press boxes are provided they tend to be in uneasy proximity to the crowd. This means that most of the reporter's time is taken up with answering questions about the half-time score at Murrayfield, and why doesn't *The Sunday Times* print more about boxing?

Worse, this lays a reporter open to abuse and even physical assault from irate members of the crowd. The Midlands breed a special type of spectator who makes a habit of sitting next to the Press box and keeping up his own running commentary.

There used to be a man at Northampton who always breathed beer fumes down the back of my neck and said loudly, 'Yer don't really *know* anything about it, do yer now? Go on, tell me, 'ave yer ever really played the bloody game?' He would then lean over my shoulder, read what I had written, and read it out aloud for the benefit of the entire stand, together with comments of his own on my literary ability.

Telephoning a report can be fraught with similar hazards. Since this often has to be done from a corner of the pavilion, one is liable to be bellowing vicious criticisms of a player with the man himself standing two feet away.

It is an unnerving experience. 'And what can one say of Blackheath's front-row query end paragraph' one shouts above the din of the bar. 'The kindest thing to say is that if they had any more guts they'd be half-hearted, exclamation mark end quotes. New par and the biggest offender was Smith who continually buckled in the tight, and who was distressingly slow about the field in the loose, so that at times he reminded one of a particularly slow Zombie, I will spell that, ZEBRA-OSWALD-MIKE – yes, Mike as in Green – BAKER-ITEM-EASY full stop new par.

'But worse was to come. Five minutes from the end Smith missed a simple pass near the —'

At this moment the wretched reporter becomes aware that a sixteen-stone man with no forehead is staring fixedly at him from two feet away, his attention attracted by hearing his name amidst the gibberish. It is Smith, backed up by another four forwards.

What happens then varies. Sometimes the frantic reporter brilliantly changes his views in midstream and compiles a paragraph of eulogy on Smith off the cuff as it were. On other occasions he grits his teeth and carries on with a group of players crammed round his shoulders, hooting and jeering if not actually seizing the phone and shouting '—— off' down the mouthpiece, much to the surprise of the copy-taker at the other end.

Sometimes the reporter sneaks off to a public call-box outside the ground. Unfortunately this frequently means that the report is phoned with people pulling open the door and shouting 'Hurry up can't yer' and similar insults not calculated to improve the quality of the literary composition.

The legend that reporters don't bother to watch the game probably arises from that most unhappy of rugby journalists, the freelance who is reporting the match for half-a-dozen different papers. What with coping with twelve phone calls, two note-books and a half-witted messenger boy, he never lifts his head to see what's going on, kind-hearted colleagues supplying him with verbal descriptions of the various scores. To add to his miseries, he is trying to describe a game simultaneously for a Coventry paper and a Swansea paper, with appropriate bias in each report.

Right at the bottom of the journalistic ladder, come the club's own tame press representatives, charged with the duty of compiling a report for the local weekly paper, which will otherwise print nothing but soccer news. They flourish especially in London, where the dreary suburban press hardly makes even a pretence of an interest in rugby. To take on this post is the fastest way to becoming the most unpopular person in the club (except perhaps, the team secretary). The road to ruin is aided by the newspapers' habit of cutting out vital parts of the report and topping it with a totally misleading headline.

The sole compensation of the job is that it does enable one to pay off old scores, which is why a club Press correspondent should always be changed in the close season. Otherwise his last report is liable to be a personal vendetta against the whole team, probably suggesting that if *he* were in charge of the club, all would be well, and including a sinister reference to the need for a complete overhaul of the club's administration.

Indeed, I knew one Press representative who, after quarrelling with his club when they dropped him from the third team, resigned, but continued to send in his reports to the local paper. Somewhat naturally, these grew more and more bitter but the newspaper refused to stop printing them. The situation was only resolved when the club's solicitor saw the sports editor and pointed out that the criticisms now verged upon the libellous. In consideration for a reasonable report, the club agreed to take the man back into the third team where he successfully ruined the fixture list for many a year.

K is for . . .

Kicker

Some rugby statistician once worked out that 53 per cent of the points scored in the game came from kicking. My own view is that 53 per cent of the points scored are much more likely to come from cheating or the other team's mistakes, but that's another matter. What is certain is that although rugby is theoretically a handling game, it is still heavily slanted towards its football origins.

There are *four* different ways of scoring with a kick – a penalty, drop goal, conversion, and goal from a mark. But there's only one way of scoring by running, and that is the try. And it's only just over twenty years since the drop-goal counted for more than the try. Indeed, originally a try counted for nothing and only the conversion scored. When points were first introduced in 1886 a try counted one point, and it didn't become three until 1894.

A stranger to the game, reviewing this situation, might well come to the conclusion that all rugby sides would concentrate heavily on improving their kicking and that the art would be a basic requirement, like passing.

He would, of course, be wrong. Proficiency at kicking is regarded as a gift from up above, which descends on only one man in the team, usually the full-back. Any player who said at training that he didn't want to practise passing, he'd prefer to retire and try some kicking, would be hurled out on his ear.

When I was at school thirty years ago, drop-kicking was absolutely banned. Once the first XV full-back, who later played for Leicester, dropped a goal in a fit of absent-mindedness and the effect was as if he had done something obscene. We all stared in horror while the rugby master hissed at him, 'You may consider yourself dropped from the First

80

XV' and I could almost swear he added the words 'miserable youth' but I'm not sure.

Any boy who confessed to a desire to be a specialist kicker in those days would almost certainly have been told to take a cold bath every day, or whenever the evil desire overcame him.

The unpopularity of kicking may be because it's such a lonely job. No wonder place-kickers develop mannerisms. Hiller's trance-like concentration and scraping of the right boot on the left sock are well-known. Less well-known is the habit a little Welsh friend of mine had of humming to himself the National Anthem as he prepared to kick. He started his run-up at 'send her victorious' and struck the ball on the second syllable of 'Ha*ppy* and glorious' and if he ever varied the magic routine he inevitably failed.

Because a kicker is alone on the stage, so to speak, the penalties for failure are exaggerated. The groaning of 70,000 voices at Twickenham, all directed at one man, is terrible to hear. But at least top-class players are not usually abused by their own side.

Down in the Extra B, the unhappy kicker is not only insulted by his team-mates but by the other side as well, who join in with cries of, 'Blimey Vipers, you can't even score when it's handed to you on a plate,' and start pulling imaginary lavatory chains. Life can be hard for the unsuccessful kicker.

But perhaps the most terrible isolation of all is that of the man who can't kick and who makes a mark in the centre of the field, knowing he hasn't the skill to reach either touchline, even if he kicks at right-angles. This fear is best summed up in the immortal phrase of Tom Reid, Garryowen and Ireland : 'The deep and mortal dread of being found with the ball in me hands in the middle of Twickenham.' Except that the dread is equally deep and mortal on the Great West Road. No wonder the mark is unknown below third team level.

Because kicking is so neglected, most players are hardly aware of the subtle difference between the many types of kick, such as the screw-kick which floats into touch, and its opposite number which curves infield at the vital moment. There are, however, different bad kicks which will be instantly recognisable.

The most common is the Hoop-la. This is frequently seen in suburban meadows, but is not unknown at Murrayfield or Twickenham. In this, the kicker steadies himself carefully, waits until the opposition are nearly on him and then very carefully, and with tremendous force, kicks the ball backwards over his own head. With luck, his own full-back may catch it, but more often the other side get there first.

A variation of this is the Yellow Streak. It is the kick made by the team's coward, who must get rid of the ball at all costs. The kicker starts his kick even before he has received the pass, and usually strikes it with his knee, whereupon the ball soars vertically upwards while the kicker runs for cover, burying his head in his arms.

Another frequently-seen kick is, of course, the Non-Starter, in which the kicker misses the ball altogether. I've done it frequently myself and I don't know a more embarrassing thing on the rugby field. The worst of it is that the momentum of kicking swings you round and you fall flat on your back while the ball bounces tantalisingly by your side, until some opponent seizes it gleefully. The only way of dodging a storm of abuse from your own side is instantly to feign an injured ankle, but even that will probably do little to protect you.

Forwards seem to have their own special type of kick (The Grunt). It has always been a mystery to me why some sixteen stone second-row forward, with legs like young oak trees, is only capable of feebly disturbing the ball when he has to kick it. Usually the ball travels in a tiny parabola for about three feet. You would think he'd be ashamed of himself, but oh dear no. After making a kick like this most

The kicker runs for cover, burying his head in his arms

forwards give a sheepish grin and go 'Huh, huh, huh' to show that really they're not supposed to know how to kick and that it was jolly sporting of them even to try.

Place-kicking, too, has as many variations.

First, there's the Patella Fracture, in which the kicker stares mesmerised at the ball for some twenty seconds, slowly advances upon it, and then buries the toe of his boot six inches in the soil about a foot in front of it. To make matters worse, he then usually hops about on one leg voiding himself of yelps of agony, and may even retire from the field injured.

Then there's the Toppler. This isn't really a kick at all, since the ball refuses to stand up and be kicked. After the third time it falls over, the unhappy kicker is driven desperate by the jeers and groans of both sides and usually makes a wild stab at the ball as it lies at a drunken angle on the ground. Just occasionally, the ball actually goes over the bar, after describing a sort of corkscrew parabola.

If this should happen, the kicker inevitably walks back with an air of great modesty, muttering something about, 'A lot of the greatest kickers prefer to place the ball at an angle . . . no, honestly, I meant to put it like that, it wasn't an accident . . .' etc. etc. Probably the greatest importance of the Toppler which goes over is the moral effect on the opposition, who are reduced to impotent silence, varied by occasional cries of 'Gawd'.

As one who has himself had the rare distinction of completely missing the ball in a place-kick, my own favourite variation is the Gurdoink, in which the kicker charges frantically at the ball, lifts his head at the last minute and scrapes his studs along the upper surface of the ball. As I say, in moments of stress, the ball may be missed altogether, but this is a connoisseur's piece.

Mercifully the laws have long ago been changed so that the scrum-half does not have to hold the ball for a conversion, and the modern player is spared the sight of the ball skidding along the ground, accompanied by a piece of the scrum-half's ear.

I have referred to the isolation of the kicker, and in someways his loneliness resembles that of a golfer. As for the golfer, there is the same necessity for a follow-through, for keeping the head down, for teeing up properly, and for concentration at all costs. And like the golfer, the rugby kicker can be easily put off by some outside noise.

True, although a cough may ruin a £50,000 putt, it isn't likely to spoil the average conversion. And first-class players become used to the storm of jeering which, alas, comes from so many crowds.

But there are more subtle forms of disturbance. A player who isn't at all put out by the entire Cardiff Arms Park hooting at him may well be put off by the sight of the opposing hooker sticking out his tongue. Worse still, is the barracker (player or spectator) who makes a quiet but disturbing remark, just as you run up.

It's very difficult to put over a successful conversion when as you stand to attention on the touch-line someone says distinctly, 'The police have just towed away your car.'

In the lower sides the kicker may well find himself subject to somewhat cruder pressures, such as the entire opposition making funny faces at him, or turning round and bending down to reveal a row of posteriors. The shortness of the posts can be another hazard, since referees in that class of rugby invariably work on the principle that if the ball is kicked high over the posts, the side has cheated by inserting a First XV man, and the kick must be disallowed.

Fortunately, the ball is usually so under-inflated that Hiller himself would have difficulty in getting it over the crossbar, so the trouble does not arise often.

This, however, only applies to the visiting side – the home team may well keep a special kicking ball on the touch-line, which they produce for their own kicks, and then remove to its hiding-place. Attempts to borrow this for an opposition kick will be met with physical violence, or in extreme cases the custodian of the special ball (usually the touch-judge) will curl up on the ground clutching it, and defy you to get it. I must be one of the few people who has seen a touch-judge at the bottom of a ruck.

From a kicking point of view, I always think the most extraordinary thing I encountered was during a game on a park, where we had no posts at all. It was one of those parks where players have to put up portable posts, and for various reasons there weren't enough left to go round.

After playing for a short time with just a heap of coats where the posts should be we hit upon the ideal solution. Whenever a kick at goal was signalled we lifted up the posts and crossbar on the next pitch and carried them over. The kick was then taken, and the posts returned to their proper place.

The people on the next pitch were decent about it, and co-operated in every way. The only snag was that thanks to the continual delays, both games lasted for more than two hours, which is probably a world record.

K is also for . . .

Knee

A part of the human body liable to collapse under emotional stress, e.g. before the annual seven-a-side tournament, towards the end of the season (but after the Easter Tour), when a player is switched from wing-three-quarter to lock-forward, after a player is dropped from the first team, and so forth. See ankle, rib, groin etc.

L is for . . .

Letter

```
        BAGFORDSHIRE SOCIETY OF RUGBY UNION REFEREES

                      Referee Report

        Clubs are asked kindly to return this report as soon
   as possible after the game as this will help us in our
   efforts to maintain the highest possible standards of
   refereeing in this area.

   Fixture .. BAGFORD VIPERS v O ROTTINGHAMIANS

   Referee ... R. GHOUL

        In my opinion the referee was (cross out which
   does not apply):

   Excellent
   Good
   Fairly good
   Fair
   Not very good
   Bad

        Any other comments you would like to make (please
   be honest).
```

Yes, I would like to say something else. None of the
adjectives above do justice to your referee, as he was so
unspeakably abominable. We had our suspicions from the
start when he was asked to adjudicate whether the pitch was
fit for play. He walked out on to the pitch, which was
covered in snow, skidded on a patch of ice, was helped to his
feet, and then had the impudence to say it was in perfect
condition.

Our confidence in him was not restored when he stuck his
head round the dressing-room door and said, 'I shan't be
playing the new line out Law today, lads, as I don't understand it, and I expect you don't either.'

Strangely enough, we do not object to the fact that mid-
way through the second half he sent off one of our front-row

The impudence to say it was in perfect condition...

for persistently using his elbow as an offensive weapon. This player has not paid his subscription for three years and would not have been selected but for the fact that we were rather short, as many players had gone to the wedding of what used to be the club cert. What we do object to is the fact that your referee refused to believe that the offending player had given the correct name. I do assure you that his name really *is* Edgecombe Downes-Golightly.

Furthermore, not only did your man refuse to believe our assurances that this was his real name, but he became completely hysterical and finally screamed in a loud voice, 'Right, if you won't tell me his real name I'll send every b---- off the field!' With which he suited action to the word. This was particularly unfortunate as we were leading 12–3 and had a good chance of recording our first home win since the end of last season. Mr Edgecombe Downes-Golightly's offer to procure his birth certificate was refused.

Finally we want to know *what happened to my gold filling?*

This fell out of my tooth before the game. As our pavilion has recently been subject to a series of thefts (believed to have been made by an aggrieved former player) it was handed to the referee. The referee said that as he had a hole in his pocket he would hide it by burying it near the corner flag. May I point out that after the game had been abandoned we could find no trace of the hiding-place, although we were all on our hands and knees for half an hour? Presumably it is still there.

May I add that, if this were not enough, your man won the jackpot on the fruit machine and left without buying a single drink.

Signed *A. Fogg*

Hon. Sec. Bagford Vipers F.C.

(Rugby Union)

M is for . . .

Megalomaniac

Every rugby team has its own megalomaniac. Some have two or three, often including the captain. Whole XVs may occasionally be composed of them.

A megalomaniac can usually be recognised through his habit of wearing a different jersey to the rest of the team. He alleges it is the jersey of his previous club which he always hints was a good deal better than the present one.

His chief interest in life is stirring up trouble. He will begin this as soon as the team gather before a match, in the dressing-room if it's a home game or in the pub, waiting for the coach, if it's an away fixture.

His favourite wheeze is to mutter some alarming rumour into people's ears, something on the lines of, 'I hear the other side have got two professional wrestlers playing in the pack. One of them bit off a chap's ear last week. They say their stand-off is an old England player, turning out under an assumed name. The referee is his father.'

Megalomaniacs rarely have a car, or if they do they are banned from driving it, so their stream of poison will be continued in the coach, together with the suggestion that it's the committee's fault for choosing fixtures like this, we never had this trouble in my old club and so on.

On reaching the changing-room, he waits until the opposition are well within earshot and then issues a torrent of insulting remarks in a loud voice, all of them calculated to rouse the other side to a pitch of fury. A typical remark, usually aimed at the thin partition between the two sides, or at the opposition's open door, is 'I can't think why we play on this stinking little ground. They're all a lot of absolute scum here anyway.'

Having ensured that the opposition are sufficiently aroused, he switches the attack to his own skipper, making a series of insane suggestions such as 'Why don't you get the stand-off to throw the ball in at the line-out' and similar half-witted schemes.

After being rebuffed in that direction he seeks out the referee and asks that official if he would like any advice or help over the changes in the Laws.

When the game is in progress, the megalomaniac distinguishes himself by picking a quarrel with a player on the other side who probably hasn't even touched him. If he can't find a player, the touch-judge will do. This ensures a thoroughly unpleasant and embarrassing afternoon for everyone, as the true megalomaniac never lets a good quarrel die down, worrying at it throughout the match, and probably half the evening as well.

Needless to say, he manages to get on the wrong side of the referee in grand style, questioning every decision and asking 'What was that for, sir?' with a world of contempt in the word 'sir'. Among other charming habits of the megalomaniac are kicking anyone who tackles him and holding the jersey of a player chasing the ball. He is the Great Obstructionist, wandering about the field apparently aimlessly, but invariably between the opposition and the loose ball.

Far from fading away with the end of the game, which thanks to his efforts usually ends in defeat, the megalomaniac becomes even more prominent after it. His activities usually start as no-side is blown when he refuses to cheer the other side and probably comes to blows with the touch-judge. In the dressing-room he analyses why his side were defeated and reaches the conclusion that everyone was to blame except himself.

He refuses to join in the beer kitty on the grounds that the other side will share it: and in any case he tends to drink peculiar mixtures like Pernod and lemonade. He frequently carries a musical instrument with him, such as a mouth-organ, which he will play until it is physically torn from his grasp. He will insist on bellowing bawdy songs with women present, and will probably strip naked, too.

His final gesture is to announce on the coach that he has committed some act of supreme larceny, such as stealing the opposition President's watch. Often the coach has to turn back to deliver his loot.

Every week the despairing captain promises he won't play the megalomaniac again, and every week, he's always there. It is impossible to ban him from the side as he just turns up knowing there will be a gap somewhere.

Eventually, he stops playing. But your megalomaniac doesn't just gradually fade away like most players. He suddenly fails to turn up one week and is never seen again, leaving behind him three years' unpaid subscriptions. Possibly he may be heard of later, playing for another club and wearing his old jersey. If he does announce his farewell to a club, it will be in the form of a rude letter to the secretary, complaining that the club is run by a clique.

The irritating thing about megalomaniacs is that, whereas ordinary club players are forgotten within a few years, they always become a club legend. The man who was violently detested when playing, becomes in retrospect a hero. Young players are regaled with stories like, 'You wouldn't remember Sid . . . he was a mad beggar . . . when we played Vipers he set fire to the referee's clothes after being sent off . . . we don't get characters like that any more.'

It's really all rather sad. The tame megalomaniac only achieves the recognition he has been seeking when he's no longer around to appreciate it.

N *is for . . .*

Notice Board

One way of judging the character of a rugby club is by its notice board. In this connection it is worth noting that the more badly a club is doing, the more notices it puts up, like the military men in the Chinese proverb who put out more flags. I don't think Northampton and Harlequins have a notice-board at all but you can hardly enter the pavilion for propaganda at the club down my road, who are in the middle of their worst season for twenty years.

Heading a notice board are, of course, the team lists, although some clubs don't bother to post up lists of players selected. They are probably wise, because the mass of crossings-out makes the lists unreadable anyway. They are also liable to be defaced by rude inscriptions from aggrieved players, who after being dropped down a side or two might scribble 'Get stuffed' after their names, or even add 'swine' against the name of the player selected to replace them.

In addition, the captain has a tendency to work from the team lists before a match, although the list by Saturday bears no resemblance to the proper side. This can cause confusion as the skipper frantically searches for players who were promoted to the Second XV on Wednesday, while weedy youths keep tapping him on the shoulder and asking if he is Stinker Jackson, because if so the team secretary told them to report to him for a game.

Next in importance to the team lists, comes a copy of the current club Newsletter. This would make the late Goebbels himself weep with envy at its smooth falsity, the way in which the hideous truth is concealed. A typical extract reads something like this:

FIRST XV REPORT BY THE CAPTAIN

'Recently an unfortunate habit of *moaning* has developed in the Club. Moaning is contrary to the tradition of rugby football. In future anyone heard MOANING will be dropped from the team immediately, no matter who he is. (*That is a veiled threat to the vice-captain, who has been complaining bitterly all season that he never gets a pass*).

'True, the First XV has not quite swept all before it this season, having lost eleven out of twelve matches. But many opponents have told us what a good game they had. Five of our eleven defeats were by fewer than twelve points, and although on three occasions we went down by fifty points, in each match we scored a very good try towards the end of the game, which shows what we can do when we get the chance.

'I feel the side has the potential to score points. The snag is we never get a fair crack of the whip because the opposition are too busy scoring themselves. If only we could sort that out, I'm sure we should storm towards victory. Meanwhile, lads, let's have no more MOANING. Moaning is as bad as coaching, both are ruinous to this great game of ours.'

Probably there will also be a newspaper cutting of last week's defeat, a poster for the next hop, and some optimistic pronouncements from the Rugby Union, twelve months out of date, offering advice, help, training courses, films, coaching and various warnings about the game, none of which anyone in the club has the slightest intention of heeding.

The official notices will be completed by a series of despairing, scribbled appeals from various sub-commitees begging players not to wash their boots in the hand-basins, to return their glasses to the bar, not to park on the pitch, to pay their subs and above all to sell tickets for the annual draw.

The more interesting part of the board, however, will be the private sector. This is frequently headed by a newspaper cutting which describes some vandalism by the third team which ended in a magistrate's court. The socially-minded in the club have probably stuck up notices for their private obsession, asking if anyone is interested in forming a squash

D

section, trying to raise a party to go skiing or getting up a group to visit *The Mousetrap* after the match against Richmond Thirds. The club megalomaniac will undoubtedly have posted up an announcement for some weird group, advertising a concert of Icelandic folk-music or demanding justice for the Kurds.

And then come the personal appeals, notices which often reveal some hidden tragedy. What can one make of this message, seen on a club notice board in the Home Counties?

FOR SALE, DINNER JACKET AND TROUSERS, VERY CHEAP. WORN ONCE ONLY (AT CLUB DINNER). JACKET NEEDS SLIGHT REPAIR WHERE OWNER FELL ASLEEP WITH LIGHTED PIPE IN POCKET. TROUSERS STAINED BY RASPBERRY TRIFLE BUT WOULD CLEAN UP A TREAT.

Sometimes there are adverts offering complete sets of rugby kit. These have to be read in conjunction with the team lists, where the vendor's name may be found in the Extra C, crossed out savagely and with a rude comment by it. Other items in the For Sale columns might include a motor car, the euphorious description of which is spoiled by the fact that someone has written at the bottom 'It's been a wreck since the Easter Tour.'

My old friend Slasher Williams once posted up a notice asking for information about his wife. She vanished suddenly, leaving no message behind, and Slasher reckoned that as the only men she knew were rugby players she must have gone off with one, probably someone she met at the clubhouse on Saturday night.

He got her back too, complete with a second-row forward from Hertfordshire who moved into his house, where Slasher was confined to one room. A cutting of the subsequent divorce proceedings was also posted on the notice board in due course. As it was the only time in his life he had seen his name in a newspaper, Slasher was very proud of this.

'Seen my story in the *News of the World*? he used to ask visitors. 'That's my wife, that is in that picture. Ripe old bag she were too.'

In the end the committee made him take the cutting down as they felt it was denigrating the image of the club.

Perhaps the saddest notice of all, though, was the one seen on a clubhouse in a remote part of Kent. It ran as follows:

VISITING TEAMS ARE ASKED NOT TO STEAL THIS NOTICE BOARD AS A SOUVENIR BECAUSE IT IS COVERING A DAMP PATCH ON THE WALL.

O is for . . .

Officials

The interesting thing about a rugby club is that while it can function perfectly well without any players (you don't *have* to play any matches to remain in existence and flourish), it grinds to an immediate halt without its hordes of officials. The best example of this is during a long spell of frost, when every game may be cancelled for more than a month. Despite the fact that no rugby is being played most clubs flourish better than ever, the pavilion being full of cheerful, thirsty people, some of whom are rather relieved that there isn't any rugby to interrupt their social life.

To become a rugby club official with a name printed in the fixture card, is not difficult. It is more difficult to avoid becoming one. The slightest hint in the clubhouse that a player wouldn't mind occasionally helping is enough for him to be seized by the appropriate sub-committee.

That is, providing the task concerned is something mundane. One of the problems of staffing a rugby club is that all the glamour committees, such as that running the bar, are vast, swollen bureaucracies, while the humdrum ones (e.g. fund-raising, Saturday teas) are only kept going by one or two dedicated people. My own experience is that the chief trouble on the bar committee is keeping people *off* it. 'Do you ever have any vacancies for extra helpers behind the bar?' they murmur, looking enviously at the row of whisky bottles. 'I've often fancied myself as a barman. I reckon I could pull a pretty nifty pint.'

If such casual offers are accepted, the new recruit will arrive full of enthusiasm for his intial duty. His first act is to pull a pint for himself after which he tends to consider that he has worked enough. His cronies will gather at his end of the bar, effectually blocking it off from other customers, and a work study will reveal that during the whole evening he serves no one but his immediate friends and himself, most of the drinks being on the house.

At closing-time he will condescend to wash an occasional glass, but all the time his eye is glancing towards the door, which soon opens an inch or two furtively, and a file of his friends tip-toe back into the bar to be served after-hours drinks.

The weirdest help I've ever encountered on a rugby bar committee was a non-smoking Welsh teetotaller of strong religious convictions, whose sole object (although we didn't know it at the time) was to sabotage the sales of strong drink.

'This won't do you any good, you know,' he used to say in his sing-song voice as he served a pint, usually short measure into the bargain. 'Puts on weight, makes fat in your vital arteries, kills you ten years too soon. Knew a man in the Rhondda who died at twenty-three from a stone in the kidneys. All due to beer. Turns to stone directly it hits the kidneys. Nasty way to die, too. How would you fancy a great stone on your kidneys, kiddo? Well, drink this pint and you'll find out.'

Strangely enough, he was the quickest server we ever had, but he succeeded in halving the bar takings in a fortnight. His master-stroke was a suggestion that beer and spirits caused impotence, which drastically slashed the consumption of the younger players.

But if the bar committee is the most popular, the fund-raising committee comes way down the bottom of the charts. Joining it is the quickest way to lose friends and fail to influence people.

'My God, not you again?' greets the unfortunate committee member vainly flogging round his draw tickets, together with an appeal to support the annual dance. After a few weeks of this, the wretched man makes the fatal mistake of buying all the tickets himself. It is significant that the entire personnel of the fund-raising committee changes every year, except for one dedicated member who has over the years reduced himself to financial ruin by purchasing draw tickets, dance tickets, tombola tickets, raffle tickets, deeds of covenant and two dozen copies of the official history of the club.

Pavilion and ground committees are bodies to be avoided. Membership of them brings no social problems (as in the case of the fund-raising committee), but tends to involve the participants in endless physical toil of the most strenuous kind. This is usually heralded by a hopelessly optimistic appeal on the notice-board or in the club newsletter asking for volunteers to turn up one Sunday morning to paint the pavilion. By eleven-thirty the only people present are three of the ground or pavilion committee. By some error no paint brushes have been provided but two old ones are found in the groundsman's hut. Work starts with these, hampered by the traces of whitewash which still adhere to the brushes.

After half-an-hour a small group of members arrives, waiting for the bar to open. They spend this interval standing behind the painters and jeering at their efforts with comments like, 'You can see old Charlie's never painted anything in his life before . . . what colour's that Charlie? . . . looks as if it's caught some sort of disease . . .'

By one o'clock the painting party is the star show of the day, with far more spectators than the First XV ever attract to a match. At this point the paint runs out and gratefully the three painters retire to the bar, promising themselves they'll come back and finish the job next Sunday.

I write with some feeling on this subject for when I was elected to the Ealing committee many years ago, my first job was to turn up one Sunday morning to dig foundations for the new pavilion. Well we dug and dug and dug and I nearly ruptured myself, but in the end we made good progress, and agreed to come back next Sunday. When we turned up, however, we were informed that we had dug the foundations *in the wrong place*. Voluntary work was abandoned after that and we got the contractors in, although the physical damage caused to certain members by the digging was never fully repaired.

Probably the most skilled task of all the officers is that of fixture secretary. The first qualification for this is an ability to project one's personality five years ahead. The unhappy fixture secretary lives permanently in the future, in 1972 dealing with the fixtures for 1976, despite his grave doubts that the world will last that long, or if the world does, he won't.

It is this strain of living in the future that makes the job so nerve-wracking, arranging fixtures for the next decade, all the time with a little vulture on the shoulder whispering, 'I wonder whether you'll live to see that fixture . . . You'll certainly be totally bald by then . . .'

To make matters worse, the fixture secretary is expected to be able to guess what the standard of the opposition will be four years hence. He's supposed to *know* that one's oldest opponents will cease to be worth playing in three years or that the Casuals are going to be a first-class club by then.

And as if that was not enough, the poor chap is then used as a scapegoat for defeat, the argument being that he shouldn't have arranged such a strong fixture. Not that that stops some people complaining he doesn't try hard enough to get a fixture with Cardiff.

By comparison with the fixture secretary, the general secretary has an easy task. The job is simply what he makes it, and if he wants a quiet life he can usually delegate most of the worries to such unfortunates as the chairmen of the sub-committees.

By the time he's passed on responsibility for things to the match secretary, team secretary, colts' secretary, bar secretary, pavilion sub-committee, ground sub-committee, ladies' sub-committee, social sub-committee, fund-raising sub-committee, hon. treasurer, chairman, President and the assistant secretary, a rugby club secretary can afford to sit back and take the credit. He will probably get a plaque in the pavilion when he dies, which is more than his gibbering underlings will ever get.

While the treasurer can't delegate any of his responsibilities, he is fortunate in that a balance sheet can be made to prove anything and he may work undisturbed until some one discovers that the bank are not honouring the club cheques anymore.

Club chairman is a greatly under-estimated post. The chairman not only does more work than most officials, but as figure-head of the club he has to take most of the criticism. He also has to spend more on drinks than anyone else. He is only remembered in a bad season ('That was when Charlie Smith was chairman ... terrible record we had') and never in a good one ('Yes, that was a great year ... Sid Jones was skipper then'). A thankless task indeed.

President is a more promising job, because the President can do as much or as little as he likes. Some Presidents are the mainspring behind the club. Others are never seen at all, especially in a bad season. Speaking as the President of a club myself (University of Surrey, and don't worry lads, I'm coming down any day now), the thing that is worrying about the job is that it is always associated with being old. To the young player all Presidents look men of incredible age. Although I regard myself as a particularly hale and hearty man in his mid-forties I am sure that if a ballot was taken among members of the Surrey University club as to whether their President could still father a child, the result would show a considerable split of opinion.

Another snag is that it is presumed that the occupants of the Presidential seat have unlimited incomes. Speaking as a President myself, I have never understood why it should be his particular privilege to buy wine for the top table at the annual dinner, especially when half the guests there are old enemies of his. Some Presidents, of course, don't, leaving the honoured guests desperately turning their glasses upside-down and tapping their noses at the wine waiter.

One last official must not be forgotten – the Vice-President. There are two sorts of vice-president – the honorary sort and those who are elected because the club needs their money. But one difficulty is common to both classes – nobody knows

A team of vice-presidents taking over the Extra B...

who they are, or even why they were elected in the first place.

If an out-of-town vice-president turns up in a pavilion and introduces himself, it causes tremendous embarrassment, with everyone standing around in pained silence trying to find a topic of conversation and muttering 'What the hell does that old fool want here?'

Yet it's impossible to resign as a vice-president. I've tried it – you can't. Whereas if you just stop sending a sub as an ordinary member, eventually a snooty letter arrives expelling you, the vice-president keeps getting hints about how sorry they were not to hear from him and how much they value his ten guineas.

I can think of only one certain way of losing the post of vice-president, and that is to exert one's rights as a member and insist on playing. A team of vice-presidents taking over the Extra B and carrying their walking-sticks into the line-outs might bring a club to its senses.

P is for . . .

Players

The most terrible result of the introduction of 'new wave' rugby into Britain in the sixties, with its coaching, planning, team training and deep thinking, has been the virtual elimination of the extremes of physical and mental ability that used to characterize the average group of rugby players.

The rot is reaching down even to the Extra C which always used to be noted for the utter extremes represented by its players – seven foot skeletons yelping pitifully on the wing, elderly dwarfs communicating in grunts during the line-outs. The appearance in such a motley crew of a new man who had never played rugby before, and who had to leave the field to adjust his truss, caused little surprise.

Today, even in the third team, it is difficult to hide anyone who doesn't know the rules, and first-class teams have the same problem in tucking away an injured man. The days when some recruit from the local soccer club could be secreted on the wing are passing. What is the use of a winger who doesn't know what line-out signals are? And whatever has happened to that haven for older players, full-back?

I look back with pleasure on many an afternoon on some sodden field, leaning against the post and swapping jokes with the soccer goal-keeper behind me, while the Extra B battered away in the distance. Occasionally I would break away from my conversation to boot the odd ball into touch, before returning to resume the chat. Indeed, an old friend claims that on one occasion he played full-back simultaneously for two teams who were occupying adjacent pitches, filtering from game to game as the situation demanded.

Today's with-it full-back, however, holds the busiest position on the field. When not in defence he's expected to be the spearhead of the attack, and the last straw has been the curb on touch-kicking which means he spends most of the afternoon following up his own kicks. It won't be long before you're too old to be a full-back at 25.

From the physical point of view this means the end of the old full-back, who was usually a pensioned-off fly-half of some thirty-five summers, still quite fast over five yards but otherwise moving at a gentle trot, and his replacement by a fervent lad who keeps complaining the threequarters can't keep up with him.

But nowhere has the change been more marked than at forward. Your old type of forward not only played differently from the backs, he *looked* different.

Front-row men had square bodies and heads, the latter occasionally coming to a point at the top. They moved on two stubby projections, and frequently on all fours. From time to time they emitted loud grunts and sometimes spoke simple phrases like, 'Why don't you —— off, ref?' or 'I'll fix you at the next line-out'. They were not supposed to handle the ball at all, and if they did so their clumsy efforts would be greeted by roars of patronising laughter.

Despite their strength, they had a habit of anticipating non-existent opposition, and on receiving a pass, had only one tactical move – they turned their vast posteriors to face the enemy, clutched the ball to their stomachs, and cringed. They would be quite capable of doing this ten yards from an undefended line.

My ideal of the old-time forward was Gnasher Brown, who said he used to play for Nuneaton, but who was shuffling around Victoria Park, Leicester, when I met him.

Gnasher had no teeth. But unlike most people, he had no false teeth either. A man of simple intelligence, he believed that Nature's ways were best and ate with his gums, which over the years had become hardened to an incredible degree. This was, he told me, partly due to the example of his father, who had one leg. His earliest childhood memory was of his mother rubbing his father's stump with turpentine to harden

They turned their vast posteriors to face the enemy, and cringed

it and the capacity of human flesh to harden into iron had impressed itself up on his mind ever since.

Besides eating with his bare gums, Gnasher used them on the field of play. Not to bite (he was a fair player, if rough). No, Gnasher actually used to tackle opponents with his mouth. Upon entering a maul (or loose scrum as it was called in those days) he would open wide his mouth and firmly fix his toothless jaw on the arm of some opposition player with such firmness that the startled player would be rendered helpless.

Those who experienced his grip told me that apart from the vice-like hold, which would reduce a limb to tingling paralysis, the ghastly rubbery feeling of the gums induced a mental effect that caused a shudder every time the incident was recalled.

Behind the old front-row used to be two lanky louts who formed the second row of the three-two-three formation, and behind them were three slightly more literate louts who formed the back row. The back row were allowed to pass and run but were bitterly criticised for not pulling their weight in the tight if they overdid the open work.

I wonder what Gnasher would say to today's front-row forward, supposed to run, dummy, swerve and sidestep with the best of them. Not to mention clever tricks like long over-head passes. Gnasher never passed in all his life. And any young forward who was so rash as to do so would receive his stern rebuke, 'Yo want to leave thet sort of stoof to they bloody backs, kiddo . . .'

Even the sacred scrum, which might still be considered the preserve of brute force, has become a matter of angles of incidence and thrust dynamics.

'In my opinion,' says today's front-row man, 'we lost because the angle of thrust was distorted by the fulcrum effect of George Smith packing at the wrong angle.'

Or as Gnasher would have put it, 'Yo had yo head right up moi arse yo daft idiot.'

So much for the pack. What of the threequarters, once the intellectuals of rugby, with a strong aversion to physical contact of any sort? They were delicate plants, frequently with University degrees, and usually from the upper or middle-classes. Here the wheel has swung right round, and the modern back is now expected to *scrummage,* or at least to invite the tackle and slip the ball back in the subsequent ruck. The result is that whereas the old-style threequarter looked like one with his creased trousers and his hair cream, today's backs all look like perfect second-row forwards.

The mind boggles (whatever that means) at the thought of someone telling the old-fashioned threequarters actually to invite a tackle, when they spent their whole lives training to avoid them.

The result of all this has been the gradual development of an all-purpose player on the lines of the Fijian side, where the only difference between backs and forwards is that the forwards are faster. Soon every player will be able to run, ruck, scrummage, sidestep and drop-kick.

Mercifully, it is still impossible to conquer Nature completely. Down in the fourth team bald, square-headed men are still seen not only in the front-row, but in the three-quarter line as well; arrant cowards, lily-livered youths and sexual deviationists still patrol the wings on countless public parks, and grandfathers are yet to be seen at full-back. Long may it be so.

Q is for . . .

Quiz

Here is a simple rugby quiz. You will probably find it easier to complete the answers if you are drunk. Some answers are given at the end of the quiz. No guarantee is offered that they are the correct ones. No prizes are offered for any solution although failure to answer any of the questions can be taken as a compliment rather than otherwise.

GENERAL KNOWLEDGE

1. The game of rugby was originated by (a) William Webb Ellis (b) Attila the Hun (c) J. B. G. Thomas.
2. The England team is selected by (a) Taking random names from the telephone directory (b) Using a crystal ball (c) A computer.
3. How many times has England beaten Wales without (a) Cheating (b) An act of God (c) An unprecedented series of lucky incidents (d) A crooked referee.

PROBLEMS FOR CLUB OFFICIALS

1. You are the club bar secretary. The police have already warned you about noise and late drinking. Ten minutes after closing time a visiting player asks for a pint and when refused says, 'It's all right, I play for the Met. Police.' What do you do?
2. As President you are presiding at the club's annual dinner when you realise that your chief speaker, a leading Rugby Union official, has risen to speak with his trousers undone. Do you (a) Bow your head in your hands (b) Nudge him and tell him (c) Do nothing (d) Stand up and undo your own trousers.
3. You are fixture secretary of a London suburban club,

three of whose sides are due to play Finchley. An hour before the kick-off, you are astonished to see two coaches from Leighton Buzzard enter the ground. Upon checking the fixture card, it says that Leighton Buzzard are next week's opponents. You have made a ghastly error. Do you (a) Leave hurriedly (b) Shoot yourself (c) Resign (d) Get out the car and drive to Leighton Buzzard.

REFEREES' PROBLEMS

1. A player falls on the ball just inside the 25 and you accidentally blow up for a try. Do you (a) Shout 'Play on' (b) Award a try (c) Invent an imaginary offence and run up shouting 'No more of that, Vipers.'

2. A high penalty kick goes over the top of a post. One touch-judge lowers his flag, the other raises his, the defending side shout 'Just outside', the kicking team shout 'Well done Jack.' Do you (a) Award a goal (b) Disallow the kick (c) Ignore the whole thing (d) Jump in the lake.

3. A seven-foot, sixteen-stone Welshman, the idol of a hostile crowd of 10,000 has just committed his thirteenth serious foul in succession after previously being warned eleven times. Do you (a) Do nothing (b) Send him off (c) Issue another warning (d) Warn someone else.

4. The captain of the home side comes up to you and says rudely, 'Ref, you are a silly ——.' Do you (a) Say 'You are a silly —— yourself.' (b) Ignore him (c) Award a penalty against him (d) Smile (e) Scowl.

ANSWERS

GENERAL KNOWLEDGE

1. (b) Although William Webb Ellis is credited with having originated the game by picking up the ball at Rugby, no

one but Attila the Hun could have invented other aspects of the game, notably the scrum.

2. It is not known how the England side are selected. Probably a combination of all three methods.

3. According to my Welsh friends, England have never beaten Wales without the intervention of at least one of these occurrences.

PROBLEMS FOR CLUB OFFICIALS

1. Arrest him. Far from putting you right with the Law he will have just the opposite effect. If there is one thing a policeman can't stand it's another policeman who plays rugby. He is suspected of getting off Saturday duties in order to turn out.

2. (*c*). Don't worry, it will provide the only laugh of the evening.

3. (*d*). On arriving at Leighton Buzzard go speedily to their clubhouse and on entering say loudly, 'Where is our opposition?'. On being told the home side have left for London, say it really is too bad, they shouldn't do these things, etc. etc.

REFEREES' PROBLEMS

1. (*c*). Have the courage of your convictions and lecture both teams sternly, without revealing what the imaginary offence was supposed to be.

2. (*c*). If either side should complain remind them it is no part of the referee's duties to keep the score. If it is a first-class match leave it to the Press to decide whether the kick went over. If it isn't, it doesn't really matter anyway.

3. (*d*). Pick on the man who is the victim of the foul, say loudly 'You provoked that' and point towards the dressing-room threateningly. Although this is a travesty of justice it will ensure that you are not black-listed by the club and that

the game can go on. One may even acquire a false reputation for great wisdom.

4. (*d*). While smiling at him, make a mental reservation to disallow any try, conversion, or penalty kick he may score. If possible, stick a few shillings on your expenses as an insult fee.

R is for . . .

Religion

If a man is seen on his knees during a game of rugby it does not necessarily mean that he is unfit; he may well be praying. Indeed, it can be stated categorically, that no other game in the world brings out such a deep religious streak as rugby.

The prayers are deep and fervent. The name of the Lord is continually being invoked aloud, but the most sincere prayers are the silent ones, delivered in the privacy of a heaving scrummage, and usually asking for mercy. Something like : 'Oh Lord, let this game end soon. I deeply repent me that I have been such a wicked person, especially as, judging by the way the blood is pounding in my ears, I may well drop dead on the pitch like old Charlie Jones did three years ago.

'Oh Lord, may I not drop dead on the pitch like Charlie Jones. May thy servant the referee be moved to blow his bloody whistle and end all this misery so we can get into the showers and after a few drinks get at the women, but if it would stop me dropping dead like old Charlie Jones then I am willing to give up the women this Saturday Oh Lord . . .'

This prayer is usually terminated by the worshipper realising that the scrum is long finished and he is alone in the middle of the field on his hands and knees. It is also frequently made after missing a tackle, especially if a long chase has been involved. I call it 'The Boozer's Prayer'.

While prayers for the game to finish – whatever the result – are the most common (in sevens one can almost see them ascending in showers), there are several other forms, of which a favourite is the Prayer Maledictory.

In this, the Lord is asked to smite either the other side or some particular member of it. I know many older players who swear that a good pray is more effective than a crash tackle. Something on these lines :

'Oh Lord, let the whistle blow for a forward pass. But if in thine inestimable wisdom Thou should decide not to perform this miracle, then let the dirty stinking rat put his foot into touch, and if in doing so he should break a leg, so much the better . . .'

The above examples are not the prayers of habitually religious people, but there is one large section of the rugby community whose prayers on the field are genuine, fervent, and completely sincere, and that is the Irish Catholics. When an Irish Catholic prays on the field, he doesn't do it furtively and silently, but rolls his eyes, raises his arms and calls to Heaven in a loud voice, 'Oh God, come down and blast these bloody Protestants . . .'

Not only does he really mean it, but he's quite convinced his plea has floated upwards successfully on the Guinness fumes, and any priest present would confirm this to be so. Having convinced himself his prayer *must* be heard, he returns to the fray with renewed vigour, using his fists as instruments of Divine Judgement.

Non-Conformists are much less prone to prayer on the pitch, but plenty of them (especially the Welsh) like to indulge in nasty, sneaky prayers *before* the game, asking only that the Lord's will be done, especially if it happens to mean victory for their team.

This idea, of course, that rugby and religion are somehow intermingled is not confined to the Welsh. The Rugby Union itself always gives the impression that while the Devil invented Rugby League, the Lord chose the Rugby Union as his own special game and probably referees occasionally in that greater Twickenham on High.

Perhaps this attitude is quite understandable in a game where the threat of serious injury or physical ruin is ever-present, especially to the more elderly player. The beliefs (or lack of them) of the most confirmed atheist must begin

'Oh Lord, let this game end soon'

to crack when he sees the opposition pack hurtling down upon him, or feels that pounding of the heart and constriction of the throat that precludes his half-time bout of retching. It is a bold man then who can resist a rugby prayer.

R *is also for* . . .

Rugby League

A game played by thirteen players each side, apparently for the purpose of providing employment to television workers. Contrary to public belief, Eddie Waring is not chairman of the R.L.

S is for . . .

Spectators

'Spectator' is still a dirty word in some parts of the rugby world. Many people regard it as the great players' sport (unlike that spectators' game up North) and if the players enjoy themselves endlessly killing the ball in the rucks so much the better. There is still a faint suspicion that entertaining rugby smacks of professionalism, although these views are rarely held by club treasurers.

As with so much in rugby, there is a great gulf between London and the provinces, especially the Midlands and West. For one thing London crowds are so much smaller than those at Gloucester or Coventry, with the exception of London Welsh, who aren't really a London club at all, they're just a Welsh club who happen to play near Kew Gardens. And London clubs, while not actually banning spectators, seem to prefer members to casual watchers. To ensure complete privacy for their games, any non-member is charged five shillings to sit on a wet plank and watch his side beaten 30-nil. For a further shilling he may purchase a programme, most of which, apart from a totally inaccurate list of the two teams, is devoted to appeals for people to give money to the club.

London spectators are also much more subdued than those elsewhere, again with the exception of London Welsh. Violent emotion and partisanship is lacking. I never cease to be amazed at the self-control of the London spectator giving vent to nothing more than an occasional cry of 'Buck up Richmond' as his sides goes down by twenty points. Even dirty play brings little more than indignant cries of 'I say' as the unconscious body of the injured player is carried away.

I often think London rugby would be more interesting as a spectacle if they had crowds like those outside the capital

Any pretence of impartiality is abandoned even before the game starts

E

where any pretence of impartiality is abandoned even before
the game starts, since the visitors run on the field to insults
and exhortations to keep it clean this year.

Nothing better illustrates the gulf between the two rugby
cultures than what happens when someone is sent off. In
London everyone feels terribly embarrassed, rather as if the
vicar's trousers had come down in the middle of the service,
and the offending player leaves the field in painful silence.

Your Midland or West Country supporter, however, revels
in the whole affair. When Mike Berridge, former England
and Northampton front-row forward, was sent off at Coventry
twenty-odd years ago, someone actually spat on him as he
walked into the players' tunnel, having been booed all the
way off the field.

'And I was lucky it was only spit,' said Berridge afterwards.

But then, provincial crowds love a hate-object, usually
some old enemy who has been maiming their best players
for several years. The giant Wheatley brothers of Coventry
used to be great targets of the Leicester crowd just after the
war. During one game at Welford Road, a little man on the
terrace kept shouting, 'Come on Tigers, get Wheatley, that
square-headed bastard who's cheating in the line-out.'
Eventually Wheatley could stand it no longer and climbed
over the fence on to the terrace where he shambled about
looking for his tormentor.

Fortunately he had fled and Wheatley returned to the
line-out, where the referee had kindly held up play for him.
Somehow I can't see that sort of thing happening at the
Stoop Ground.

Don White, the great Northampton and England wing-
forward, was a favourite target for Coventry spectators, and
elsewhere too. Like Hiller (another of the men spectators
love to hate) he took a long time over his kicks and once at
Coventry he took so long that the whole crowd erupted into
pandemonium. White turned to the referee and said, 'I'm
not taking it till they're quiet.' Whereupon he sat down on

the ball and waited for silence. It took a long time but in the end the crowd shut up, and he then put the kick over.

Referees, too, receive different treatment in London. The polite groans of 'I say, ref' in the capital are nothing to the outburst that will great an unpopular decision at Newport or Bristol. The real advantage for a referee in the Metropolis, however, is that because of the impersonality of London, he is a stranger to most of the spectators.

London referees don't have to suffer the highly personalised insults beloved of Welsh crowds in particular, in which a spectator loudly reveals some secret of the unhappy man's private life, which has long been rumoured around the town. It is not easy to control a game when someone shouts loudly, 'The trouble with you, ref, is that you've been having too much on the side recently.' This will be followed by a shriek of delight from the crowd, with perhaps some further pertinent comment like 'Ask him what he was doing in Cardiff last week.'

But then, the general standard of crowd wit is lower in London. I always liked the remark of the Leicester bus-driver, when a referee left the field at half-time. He leaned over the barrier and said penetratingly, ' 'Ave yer gone to look at yer rule-book, ref?'

There are, however, two classes of spectators which are common to all grounds. One is the sadist, he-who-foams-at-the-mouth and shouts, 'Kick him off it' at the least excuse, usually when the unfortunate player is pinned under ten others. I always feel referees should be allowed to send off people like that.

The other is the elderly pensioner who's followed the game since the players wore long trousers. At Northampton you find him in the Gordon stand; in London you come across whole platoons of them at Richmond, in that little stand with the narrow slit in front.

They invariably wear black woollen mittens with no fingers and cannot afford a programme. They judge the game by the standards of 40 years ago and time becomes truncated for them, so they plaintively recall the giants of the past as if they still existed. They never remember the names of the modern players and never forget those of long ago.

Cyril Gadney, former international referee and R.U. President, tells a delightful story of two elderly spectators discussing the news from India some years ago.

'I see someone's shot Ghandi,' said one of them.

'I'm not surprised,' said the other. 'He always was a bloody awful referee.'

Of course ninety per cent of rugby games are not watched by any spectators at all, unless one counts both sets of three-quarters, staring in bored fashion at the endless scrums and occasionally waving their arms to keep their hands warm. At that level animals are the most numerous and critical spectators. Cows, as is well-known, are fascinated by rugby pitches, and the evidence is plain. Dogs enjoy joining in, and many a poodle has been savagely heeled from a ruck. I have seen a player fiercely attacked by a mastiff which resented the way he had tackled his master. Despite shouts of 'Get off, Rover, get back in your basket' Rover removed a piece of the tackler's shorts and a morsel of flesh before being dragged away and locked in the pavilion, where he howled all afternoon.

I've accused London crowds, such as they are, of being dull but they have always been civilised. Certainly the standard of spectatorship at Twickenham for international matches has declined. Once, the hush that fell on 70,000 people for a kick at goal was one of the experiences of a lifetime. Today, alas, the kicker's run-up may well be punctuated by jeering and hooting and possibly the odd toilet roll in addition. Well, it shows they're interested at least. But at times one feels that perhaps there was a lot to be said for the old London spectator with his travelling rug and his tweedy wife in brogues. He may have lacked wit, but he did have manners.

S *is also for* . . .

Soccer

It's inevitable that there should be a good deal of rivalry between soccer and rugby since they are the two main branches of football. What is not always realised, however, is that they used to be the same game. Until the second half of the last century it was all football, although played with considerable local variations. The proud title Football Club, flourished by the older rugby clubs instead of the more modern Rugby Football Club, is an indication that when they were founded football still hadn't split up so rigidly. Leicester, for instance, in their first season, played soccer one week and rugby the next, alternating the two games. Blackheath were actually founder-members of the Football Association, although they withdrew after the inaugural meeting in 1863. This was not so much because they wanted to keep handling of the ball, but because they objected to the F.A.'s insistence on banning their cherished tradition of hacking.

Incidentally, the name soccer is supposed to be derived from the slang word 'socy', a corruption of Association, to distinguish association football from the other sort.

It is usually believed that a soccer player finds rugby a difficult sport to master if he transfers. My own experience is that the reverse is true. I've played with dozens of ex-soccer players (including a Q.P.R. half-back) who took to rugby without much difficulty. My old friend Joe Pickup, President of Leicestershire R.F.U. in 1970–1, didn't begin his rugby career until he was 36. After giving up soccer, which he had played all his life, because he was too old, he was strolling round Victoria Park, Leicester, watching the soccer matches, when he happened to become interested in a rugby game on a neighbouring pitch. Within a few days he was playing for Stoneygate, a local side, and within a year or two had been capped for Leicestershire when nearly 40, eventually becoming President of the county union.

It is true, however, that the soccer player snatched off the touchline, or from between the goalposts of the next pitch (as once happened in my experience), can sometimes be an embarrassment. It is not so much that they do everything wrong, although their habit of packing down with the opposition can be disconcerting. They are usually quite all right as long as they can keep with the forwards, and will pad around happily with their new pals, provided the ball does not come loose. It is then that their newness to the game shows itself. They simply are afraid to do anything at all, and usually stand petrified.

If this happens, they will respond best to sergeant-major tactics, in which every move is shouted to them in detail.

I remember one young soccer player who received the ball on the opposition 25 with no one between him and the line. To our horror he just stood there, wondering what he ought to do, while we seethed in frustration at the chance he was missing. Suddenly the voice of our hooker, who was headmaster of a particularly tough school, thundered forth.

'Run towards the railway embankment, lad' he shouted.

The boy did so. Fortunately the railway was behind the line. Having crossed the line he halted in bewilderment.

'Turn right towards the posts, son' boomed the hooker.

The boy did so. The opposition menaced him.

'For God's sake fall over.'

The lad did so and scored a try in his first game of rugby. After that there was no stopping him. Eventually we had to take him aside and explain that the others wanted to play as well.

The plight of a rugby player in a soccer team is often

much worse. Soccer is such a universal game that it is assumed he knows the rules, despite the fact that most soccer players themselves don't, and he will receive little explanation and advice. To make matters worse, his knowledge of the game is probably based on having played it many years previously, since when soccer has changed even more than rugby.

The first shock will probably come when the skipper asks 'Would you mind playing Sweeper?' This means little to those of us who played left-half in the days when the W Formation was the latest thing on earth and goals were scored by men called centre-forwards in baggy trousers.

Tactics, too, have altered and the rugger man will find that these days people playing in defence are *not* supposed to play cards with the goalkeeper. They have to keep attacking all the time, like the modern rugby full-back.

The worst problem for the rugger man, however, is avoiding the habit of using rugby tactics. I don't mean picking up the ball and running like William Webb Ellis did – most of us can grasp that that's not allowed – but in tackling and evading tackles. I can never resist a good old-fashioned hand-off when shoulder-charged at soccer. The effects, though, are terrible – hordes of people shouting abuse and telling you to get off the field, and the referee rushing up waving his arms, blowing his whistle angrily and pointing to what the old reporters used to call 'the fatal spot'.

Actually I haven't played soccer since a fearful experience in my last game, when I was accused of fouling the goalkeeper. It seemed quite reasonable to me that if he fell on the ball and crouched on it I could try to hack it from his grasp, and if a few blows fell on his ribs, serve him right for not releasing it.

I had hardly delivered my first kick when I was dragged off the ball from behind by two other players while the goal-keeper staggered to his feet, clutching his chest, bending double, and clinging to the goal for support.

The referee would have none of my plea that in rugby the goalkeeper would have been penalised for not playing the ball. In twenty-five of years of rugby I had never been sent off but in two minutes of soccer I achieved it. The ref even took my name, although what good that did I haven't the faintest idea, unless I have been subsequently banned from soccer for life without knowing. I hope not. I still look forward to another game, only next time I think I'll look at the rules.

T is for . . .

Team Secretary

One of the great mysteries of rugby football is what makes a man become team secretary? Most administrative positions do at least involve a certain amount of power: even secretaries and treasurers are allowed to write rude letters to people who don't pay their subs or who set fire to opponent's pavilions. But the team secretary is merely the passive recipient of a torrent of evasion and abuse, a sort of pillar-box for rude communications, who's not entitled to answer back.

It is true that at the top of the tree there must be a certain satisfaction in sending out a lofty summons to someone to play for Harlequins against Cardiff, especially if you get a phone call back to say that the recipient has broken a bone in his foot but will desperately try to get fit as he doesn't want to lose his place. But that sort of situation is rare for the average team secretary. He is much more likely to have the postcard returned (unstamped) with '—— off' scrawled all over it. That is always assuming, there isn't some pathetic excuse like, 'Must be a mistake, you know I never turn out against Finchley as it involves changing trains . . .'

In some mysterious way, people who drop out after selection always seem to manage to make it appear the team-secretary's fault. Every deep-rooted and suppressed piece of venom and hatred is directed at that hapless and innocent individual simply because his signature happens to be on the bottom of the card. Men with a grievance, who are content merely to mutter in the clubhouse, will burst out against a team-secretary, often scrawling completely irrelevant *graffiti* when they return their cards, diatribes such as, 'Am not available as long as the club persist in charging two shillings for hot dogs . . .'

Yet there are always people willing to do the job. My own

theory is that they take it on because they have a deep-rooted desire to be *needed*. And by golly, they are.

Theoretically, of course, a team secretary's duties are merely to note the selection committees' decisions on Monday evening, and send out the appropriate selection cards to those picked. These are usually couched in the sternest language, informing the recipient that if he scratches after noon on Wednesday he will be instantly expelled from the club.

In practice, however, that is but the start of his troubles. He usually finishes up by personally selecting four-fifths of the players in anything up to half-a-dozen sides. Far from doing this in calm consideration during the week, the whole process has to be telescoped into an insane period between eight o'clock on Friday evening (the favourite time for dropping out of rugby teams) and three o'clock on Saturday afternoons. He may well still be at it right up to half-time, trying to persuade a coach-driver to play. The team secretary himself is expected to fill the last gap if he is under 45.

The situation in the average team secretary's home on a Friday evening really needs a skilled administrative staff of five to cope with it. Instead, there is one man, aided perhaps by a few members of his family, which leads to the ridiculous situation that half the Extra B's in this country are selected by someone's wife or mother, or even the German *au pair* girl.

Indeed, I can recollect my old club losing its unbeaten record because the team secretary was in the bathroom when the stand-off rang to say he couldn't play. His aged mother took the call, and although I forget what the player's real name was, I do know she wrote it down as 'Guggenheim'.

Faced with a message saying 'Mr Guggenheim can't play' the team secretary decided that anyone with a name like that *must* be in the fifth team, and ordered his last stand-by (an elderly crone of about 55) to substitute. The result was that, for the first time in living memory, the C XV had

Half the Extra B's in this country are selected by some-one's wife or mother

sixteen players, while the first team had to play the touch-judge, with disastrous results.

The following dialogue must not be uncommon on Friday evenings :

TEAM SECRETARY : 'Sorry I'm late, darling. I was kept at the office . . . well, I did just have half a pint on the way home. Any calls?'

WIFE : 'About fourteen. Smelly Smith has gone to Hong Kong. Dai Evans, Idris Morgan and Ivor Jones have all been struck by a sudden disease. Fred Fogg, Alf Jordan, Bert Smith and Weevil Watson are all injured; Jigger, Knocker, Chalky, Dusty and Nobby can't play; Arthur Wright is getting divorced, and Tom Brown *won't* play.'

TEAM SECRETARY : 'Won't?'

WIFE : 'Yes. He says he distinctly told you after the same game last season that they were the dirtiest crowd he'd ever met, and he'd never play them again. He says he can't understand why you didn't remember, and if this is the way the club's run, no wonder it's got such a rotten playing record.'

TEAM SECRETARY : 'What have you done?'

WIFE : 'I picked out the first fourteen names from that list of yours and phoned them to play.'

TEAM SECRETARY : 'My God! That's the list of people not allowed to play until they pay their subscription.'

WIFE : 'It doesn't matter. Only three said they'd turn out. By the way, you'll need some new laces in your boots. I put you down for the Extra A.'

The state into which a team secretary is reduced is frequently revealed by the condition of a match card sent to a player. These contain valuable clues. The presence of blood on a match card, for instance, means it was written during backfast after the sender had cut himself shaving, and the recipient, therefore, is a last-minute choice.

Teacup rings on a card indicate that the secretary's wife sent it, a sure sign that the player concerned is a substitute for someone else. Beer-stains are a certain indication that one is an original selection. They are caused during the selection committee meeting, as the team secretary scribbles away with a pint at his elbow.

Sometimes, of course, the match cards don't arrive at all, as on the occasion when our team secretary's wife, having been given the cards to post, carried them around in the car for a week, with the result that not one player out of 75 turned up on the Saturday. I think this particular official must have been prone to bad luck because on another occasion his dog ate the entire First XV front-row.

However, I did once receive a card which revealed such extraordinary confusion that I kept it as a souvenir and an example of the state to which a team secretary can be reduced.

To start with, there was a scorch mark across one corner, a nail varnish stain and a pencilled note : 'Get cat food.'

It began 'Dear Fred'. This was crossed out and 'Dear Bert' substituted, but this was also crossed out in favour of 'Dear Mike'.

It continued : 'You have been selected to play on Saturday for . . .' and on the dotted line was written 'Either the First XV, the Extra A or the Extra C'. This extraordinary statement was explained by a little footnote which said, 'Please meet at the Baker's Arms at one o'clock and if the First XV do not have a stand-off be prepared to travel to High Wycombe. But if Frank Matthews returns from Manchester, please pick up Charlie Brown at the corner of Hangar Lane, and play for the Extra C provided that Sid Hawkins does not contact you as full-back for the Extra A.'

As a final insult there was scrawled across the bottom the stock warning, 'Please be fit for this important fixture.'

In the end the First XV lost 48-nil. Not that I was there. I was intercepted at the pub door with an urgent message to pick up Jack Robinson at Kew Bridge and proceed at once to Salisbury, where the fourth team had already gone by coach. It was dark when we arrived.

U is for . . .

U.S.S.R.

Although a surprising amount of rugby is played in Eastern Europe, very little is known about it. There are teams in Czechoslovakia, Poland, Russia, Hungary and Roumania, but the Roumanians seem to be the only people with much contact with the West and they frequently visit France and Italy. A Roumanian team toured Britain about twenty years ago, and some British sides have visited there, including Harlequins, who left their mark with a memorable gaffe by a senior official at a post-match banquet.

Observing two signs on a street lavatory he concluded that the writing meant 'Ladies' and 'Gentlemen' and accordingly began his speech with those two Roumanian words as a gesture of courtesy towards his hosts. The reaction exceeded his wildest hopes. At least half the guests stood up and cheered.

Afterwards he asked a Roumanian interpreter why every-one had been so excited.

'It is the first time,' came the reply, 'that anyone here has begun his speech with the words "Urinals and Water Closets".'

But the U.S.S.R. remains the great rugby enigma. Since World War Two ended there have been at least four reports that rugby was to be re-started in Russia, and the latest news was that there are now sixty clubs there. And that is all anyone does know. No one has ever met a Russian rugby player. No news filters forth. No translation of rugby songs has appeared and the State vodka parlours are still apparently immune to the strains of Vladivostock Vera, the Soviet equivalent of Eskimo Nell.

One reason for the lack of news of Russian rugby may be, of course, due to the activities of the Secret Police, who decided that when a scrum was formed players were plotting against the Government. Or perhaps everyone has a production target of so many goals, tries, strikes against the head and so on, and those who fail are dropped or simply vanish.

Or perhaps they don't vanish. Maybe up in the howling wastes near the Arctic Circle, changing in a log hut and bathing in the snow, is Russia's biggest rugby club – Siberia Academicals, a club with a constantly-growing membership, so that now they are running forty-six teams, the lowest of which is the Extra S. And after the match, as the long Arctic night closes in, and the wolves shriek outside, the sound of balalaika is heard from the pavilion as the players, composed mainly of dissident authors and Jews, sing the saddest rugby songs on earth, interrupted by occasional shots from outside.

Perhaps eventually the Russians will realise that playing rugby is biggest form of torture on earth, and instead of the present tendency to send rebellious writers to lunatic asylums, they will receive the dreaded sentence, 'Comrade, you will be pleased to hear you have been selected for Siberia Academicals . . .'

The Russians have an understandable tendency not to indulge in sports internationally until they know they will give a good account of themselves, which probably accounts for some of the lack of foreign contact, even with Eastern *bloc* countries. It is, however, rumoured that in recent years they have played a rugby international against Communist China. Unfortunately, nobody knows who won, as the team never came back.

There is, however, a well-documented record of one international played by the Soviet Union. In 1968 their United Services visited Czechoslovakia, taking with them half a million supporters. And they liked it so much, most of them are still there.

V is for . . .

Despite periods when one is tempted to suggest it should be replaced by something more exciting such as a wheelchair race, the Varsity game still holds its mysterious attraction, as it has for nearly a century. It's not often remembered, by the way, that Conan Doyle based a Sherlock Holmes mystery, 'The Missing Threequarter' on the Varsity game. The story concerned Cambridge's crack threequarter ('Whether it's passing, or tackling or dribbling there's no one to touch him, Mr Holmes') who vanished the night before the match. Holmes got him back, but too late to save Cambridge from defeat.

The atmosphere of the Varsity match has changed somewhat from the days when well-mannered rows of prep-school boys in grey shorts and blue gaberdine macs gave vent to shrill cries on the touch-line. At times on the south terrace it feels as if every Borstal within 100 miles had given its pupils a day off. Young giants of sixteen from local schools prowl the terraces, smoking and throwing toilet rolls and apparently completely beyond the control of their masters, who go to great lengths to avoid looking at them.

But despite what people say, the university students aren't very different from their predecessors. As always they fill one with the feeling, 'God help us if those are the future leaders of politics, education and industry' but then, that feeling has persisted for centuries. And the older spectators, 90 per cent of whom never went to either or any university, remain as always totally committed to the victory of a team they originally supported on the merest whim.

There would probably be indignant cries of protest if one said that University rugby in its wider sense has only existed a short time. But it is true. Oxford and Cambridge have been dominating the scene for a hundred years but until

the fifties university rugby elsewhere in England hadn't
been of the slightest importance by first-class standards. That,
of course, did not necessarily apply in the other Home
Countries.

The enormous increase in the number of students at
Redbrick universities (most of which are built of glass), colleges of education and technical colleges has in fact forged a
completely new force in English rugby, whose potential is not
yet fully realised. As to whether Oxford or Cambridge would
thrash the living daylights out of Loughborough Colleges or
St Lukes must remain a mystery since they never play each
other and probably never will. Loughborough Colleges'
game with St Lukes has become a sort of poor man's Varsity
match, although as yet no substitute for the original.

But if Oxford and Cambridge are still supreme, the others
have made the seven-a-side field their own. Watching St
Lukes and Loughborough battle it out before 50,000 people
in the Middlesex Sevens, makes one realise the progress that
Redbrick rugby has made in the last two decades.

I always remember playing a Midland College of Art
and Technology in 1948. It was their First XV and our
club's Third. We didn't, in fact, normally play the Tech,
but then, nobody did, so they would always fill a gap when
some side or other was without a fixture.

I don't know about the technology side of the college, but
the artistic element was well represented. Three of them had
long Augustus John beards down to their waists, two of them
were holding hands and one of them actually walked on to
the field in galoshes. My own side, which consisted of some
of the most stupid and unintelligent youths in the county,
minced on to the field in imitiation of how they imagined
queers would walk. But this demonstration passed unnoticed
by the Tech, who were busy sorting out their depleted
numbers.

Not surprisingly, we established an immediate ascendancy
when the game began, partly due to our hooker's habit of

pulling his opposite number to his knees by the end of his beard in the tight scrums. Also, the Tech stand-off was hampered considerably by his galoshes.

When we were 20 points up, Jim, one of our second-row forwards, suddenly stood rigid and then fell on his back with staring eyes. The horrified college players rushed to him but our captain ran up shouting, 'It's only epilepsy. Just cover him with a coat and play round him. It's best not to touch him.'

This was quite true. We were used to Jim's fits. One could forgive the Tech, however, for being a little alarmed and they peeped in a frightened way at Jim's prone, rigid, staring figure as play went on. Then, without warning, Jim suddenly sat up, shook his head and rushed back into the game.

It was the last straw for the Tech. They looked at him as if he had risen from the dead, and one or two started crossing themselves. Not one of them could bring themselves to tackle him, so he romped round the field unopposed. At this point, the college captain created rugby history by simply capitulating.

'We've had enough,' he said. 'You're 48-nil up and bound to win, and some of my lads are complaining that they don't like to tackle that there living corpse you've got in the second-row. We give in.'

His offer was accepted instantly and the game ended. In the evening the Tech recaptured their honour somewhat by demonstrating a method of getting tight for ten shillings (beer was cheaper then), which involved switching from beer to draught cider and back again frequently. My last memory is of being thrown off a tram by the conductor because I had turned green.

Today the Tech is a vast hive of education, doubtless quite respected in the rugby world. But I hope today's students will occasionally raise a glass to the student-players of the past who kept the game alive in improbable seats of learning, galoshes and all.

V is also for . . .

Vandalism

Vandalism is the deliberate destruction of someone else's property. When carried out by a thug it is considered a serious matter. When perpetrated by rugby players it is merely high spirits, letting off steam, etc.

This sarcastic comment may seem somewhat hypocritical from one who has stood by and applauded while a large forward swung across the saloon bar of a hotel on the chandelier (which tore out of the ceiling in a sheet of blue flame). But these days the activities of rugby players can't be dismissed as the pranks of a minority of privileged lunatics. For one thing there are so many more rugby players; and for another thing there's so much more vandalism. The time when Cambridge undergraduates could pinch policemen's helmets in the Haymarket and have it all regarded as a joke has gone.

In any case, it is more the witty practical joke rather than the act of vandalism which one remembers from the Easter tour or an away game. I shall always recall with pleasure our stand-off taking over the reception desk of a hotel when the girl in charge vanished for a few moments, and booking an entire coach party of 30 people all into the same room.

It was the same man who, during the night, fixed a 'Bathroom and toilet' sign on the bedroom door of a front-row forward with the result that from six a.m. onwards he was disturbed by a stream of callers, many of whom became highly indignant and demanded to know what he meant by sleeping in the bathroom.

Unfortunately, the dividing line between team joker and

A smoke-shrouded figure slavering with rage . . .

psychopath is a narrow one, and while it may seem funny when the scrum-half is locked in the cold-store for the night, it isn't so funny when the guests find foot-marks on their breakfast bacon.

There was one act of tour vandalism, however, of which I heartily approved. We had been staying at a small hotel run by a little Welshman straight from the pages of Dylan Thomas (Larceny Evans we nicknamed him). Evans had two prices – those he charged the locals and those he charged us, and ours were considerably more. Anything other than merely sleeping was charged extra, including baths, use of television and a second cup of coffee at breakfast. The front door was locked at 10.45 p.m. prompt and when we came to depart everyone had been charged for six or seven meals they had never eaten.

Larceny Evans came to the door to see off our coach, mainly, I suspect, to make sure we hadn't pinched anything. He stood watching us drive down the street, when from behind him, in the lobby of the hotel, came the sound of a loud explosion and a cloud of grey smoke billowed out from the door.

It was the work of a young Army officer in our side, who had planted a smoke-bomb and fuse behind one of the potted ferns just as we left. The last we saw of Larceny Evans was a smoke-shrouded figure slavering with rage and waving his arms at the coach.

W is for . . .

Women

The theory that playing rugby is merely a sex-substitute may well be true; but judging from purely outward appearances it is a pretty poor substitute. Not that one need pay any attention to the ghastly charade of the club rapist with his stories of how the Cornish women fell into his arms. The man to watch is the quiet little Welsh threequarter who is saying nothing but surreptitiously holding your girl-friend's hand.

The days when a clubhouse was a masculine preserve have long gone. Leicester and Moseley were among the last two clubs to succumb and they went under years ago. Incidentally, the clubhouse was never entirely a masculine place – women were allowed in to clean up, make tea, wash up, and do similar menial tasks. It was only the interesting things like drinking and shouting songs from which they were banned.

But the young things who nowadays fill the pavilion from seven o'clock onwards when the disco starts are not really rugby women, although they may later become so, often breeding fine forwards, somewhat to their surprise when they see the monster they have reared.

Your genuine rugby woman is the wife or girl-friend who finds her whole life dominated by this wretched game. They tend to fall into three grades: interested; not interested but tolerant; and don't-you-dare-come-home-again-in-that-state.

The Interested spend hours on muddy touchlines, or in cold stands, chirping at the players and gossiping with other Interested Women. They may help with the teas and later have a drink in the bar, trying to pretend they aren't embarrassed when the club psychopath starts singing 'Little Angeline'. Sometimes they bring their children who may be seen toddling round wearing Daddy's jock strap on their heads like a hat, or else howling miserably in a corner.

As they grow older, Interested Women display alarming sadistic tendencies. Whole platoons of them can be heard squeaking against the tactics of the other side, and baying for the blood of some innocent forward who is merely getting revenge for what happened in the last line-out.

They will perform incredible feats of self-sacrifice, seeing their washing-machines burst under the overload of kit and coping with the children single-handed while Daddy's playing or training. On Saturday nights they are used to being woken up by the crash of a car hitting the garage doors, and various voices calling 'Shush' loudly. Then follows the sound of heavy footsteps downstairs, the clink of glass, and the swish of a soda syphon, whose contents, as they well know, are mostly going over the furniture.

Later comes a noise like an elephant trying to tip-toe upstairs and after an interval the ghastly sound of someone trying to pull the lavatory chain seventeen times, unsuccessfully. For the next two hours there is a continual loud drone of conversation from downstairs, punctuated by odd cries and shouts for silence, together with the noise of the lavatory cistern being pulled from its moorings.

About three there is an outbreak of bedlam as the guests depart. Heavy breathing is heard outside the bedroom door and the husband passes by, enters the wrong bedroom, and probably goes to sleep on the floor.

Those women who are not interested but tolerant, pose few problems to a player. They are never seen, except perhaps at the annual dinner-dance, where he presents them to his friends rather as one might show a mentally-defective child and then pushes her into the background. They will normally help a player in a minimal manner, e.g., they will allow him to be out till ten on Saturday but they won't wash his kit. They don't object to the Easter Tour but their husband has to take them to Brighton to make up for it.

Women of the don't-you-dare-come-home-again-in-that-state are not normally seen in the clubhouse, but their reputation somehow becomes known and can be judged from the anxious expression on a player's face when the coach makes yet another unscheduled stop at a public-house on the way home. A man's kit is often a clue to his wife's character. If he turns up with it looking exactly the same as it was when he came off the field the previous week, all is not well.

Occasionally, players with disapproving wives make the mistake of turning up with them at a club social function, either in the hope that this will soften them up or in response to a demand, 'Why should you be always going out without me?' To most people's surprise they are never as formidable as their reputation, and may even be clinging and sweet.

The women will all agree that Charlie's wife is rather charming really and why doesn't he bring her to the club sometimes? To which Charlie will reply with a mechanical laugh and a dreadful haunted stare in his eyes; his wife will reply somewhat tartly to the effect that she can never see anything in rugby, it seems such a pointless game, doesn't it disgust you to see all those men hanging on to their forgotten youth, don't you agree that men are childish, etc., etc.

Men with wives like that never last long. By thirty they have prematurely retired and spend their Saturday afternoons mowing the lawn or walking their brood. They will, however, completely deny that it is all due to their wife's influence and blame an old knee injury or pressure of work.

W is also for . : .

Whurp

Sound emitted frequently by stand-off halves, especially if playing behind a beaten pack. A cry of fear; an appeal for Divine Intercession.

X is for . . .

X-ray

Few rugby players have not at one time or another been confronted by the X-ray department of a hospital. This is often cunningly situated in a separate building from the casualty block, so that patients can be left lying in the open on stretchers while taking their turn in the queue.

Provided, that is, that the X-ray department is open at all. The impression one gains is that this particular section of the hospital operates under its own laws, and tends to keep shop hours. As early closing day is usually Saturday (Sunday being a holiday all day), injured rugby players are liable to have to wait until Monday before discovering whether their collar-bone is broken. Many a player has limped around all week-end on a broken ankle, after being told by the casualty department to take a few aspirins and come back on Monday.

I am irresistibly reminded of the plumber whose doctor refused to visit him late at night, and told him to take a couple of pills and come round in the morning if it got any worse. Some years later the doctor rang the plumber at night in great distress with a burst pipe, 'Just put a couple of aspirins on it,' said the plumber, 'and if it gets any worse, come and see me tomorrow.'

But then, the attitude of casualty departments to rugby players is scarcely friendly. While they will show the greatest sympathy to some fool who has put his fork through his foot while gardening, the arrival of a mud-stained player with broken ribs is regarded as a deliberate attempt to waste their time.

In this respect, one can at least say for the X-ray department that, if it is open, one will be dealt with skilfully and carefully. My own experience is that the X-ray people are far better at diagnosis than the casualty doctors. I shall never forget listening with mounting horror to an argument between a young doctor and the X-ray girl about my arm. The girl said the elbow was dislocated : the doctor said the bone was damaged, and wanted to pull it straight and put in plaster.

I still don't know who had won the argument when they put me under the anaesthetic. My last conscious thought was what my arm would be like when I came round. Well, it wasn't in plaster, so I suppose the girl had won her point. But it hurt so much I'm not sure the doctor didn't have a private attempt to prove his theory.

I suppose one cannot entirely blame a hospital for its casual attitude to sporting injuries. The patients are not always very co-operative. Some years ago, I was playing at Salisbury, when one of our side broke his leg. The hospital wanted to keep him in overnight, but once the plaster was on he insisted on being carried into the pub, intending to return to London lying on the back seat of the coach.

Unfortunately, half-way through the evening, he turned green and collapsed while singing Eskimo Nell, and we had to present ourselves back at the casualty department, carrying the unconscious body of our friend, and ask if they would please take him in again as he had just passed out. To say they were not pleased would be an understatement.

But where the rugby side is the apple of the town's eye, as in the Midlands, West and Wales, the position is reversed. Then, players from the home side are liable to arrive attended by the team's tame doctor, who personally brushes aside the nurse and calls for V.I.P. treatment. If there is a chance of the player returning to the game he is not only patched up hurriedly, but given pep pills and a whiff of oxygen as well, while other patients sit on dirty wooden benches and quietly bleed to death. Members of the visiting side are also given special treatment, but invariably they are warned that it would be fatal to return to play out the match.

Sometimes the team doctor's influence is inadequate on

an away game, especially in London. In that case the player is liable to awake from an operation to find the team doctor bending over him and whispering loudly, 'Don't worry old chap, I'll reset the bone myself when we get home. Charing Cross has always been a bad place for fractures . . .'

But all the idiosyncrasies and faults of hospitals pale into feeble insignificance compared with the treatment meted out to rugby players in the wartime Army, where sporting injuries were treated on the same basis as a self-inflicted wound.

Not that the Army ever encouraged anyone to report sick. The difficulty was that if one was really ill, you would be too weak to go through the ghastly routine involved in seeing the Medical Officer. As sickness was not accepted as an excuse for lying in bed after Reveille, it was a little difficult to know what to do.

A sick or injured soldier was expected to rise at 6 a.m., pack up everything he possessed in his kitbag and packs, and carry it a mile to the quartermaster's stores. This was no easy feat with appendicitis. Having missed breakfast, he would then parade at 8 a.m. in the rain and be marched a mile to the medical shack.

The march of the sick squad was rather grotesque, with the sergeant trying to keep discipline among a stumbling throng of sick men, some of whom had a temperature of 103. When the medical hut was reached the sergeant would shout, 'Smartly now – sick parade . . . Halt!' and the whole mob would shamble to a stop, while one or two of the more seriously ill collapsed insensible with low moans. Patients then queued in the open for threequarters of an hour to await the arrival of the M.O.

The Medical Officer in my unit was nicknamed Dogface, and persistent rumour had it that he had been a vet in civilian life.

His bedside manner was a trifle brusque. He usually opened the proceedings by telling the patient to stand to attention, and putting him on a charge for not shaving. He would then say, 'And now, lad, what have you been doing to yourself?' thus putting the onus fairly and squarely on the sick soldier.

Some care was needed in the reply. It was little use saying, 'I felt somewhat run-down this morning,' or 'I've not been too grand lately, sir,' unless one wanted to spend the rest of the week doubling around the square in full kit.

But a full description of all symptoms was useless, as Dogface firmly believed that all soldiers were suffering from constipation and VD. Thus, whatever the nature of the illness, a laxative would be prescribed and the wretched soldier made to drop his trousers while Dogface delivered a homily at his unhappy loins.

If no symptoms of VD were present, Dogface would say, 'You might have it without any external symptoms. Don't think you've got away with anything my lad.' The soldier would then automatically be marked fit for duty, and would go away without his original ailment ever having been discussed.

Because of the activities of Dogface, a sort of black market in medical treatment grew up in the regiment. The garrison dentist would be consulted about painful feet; a vet from the R.A.S.C. mule squadron would advise on bone injuries. In extreme cases, soldiers would travel to another town and pretend to collapse on the railway station. On being carried to hospital they would beg the doctor to do something about their fibrositis before sending them away.

Once, however, I was unable to avoid having a rugby injury treated by Dogface. It was my own fault, since I was injured falling on the ball. This was not a practice I made a habit of, and I was staring at the ball hoping something would happen when I was thrown on to it by a large Irish signals sergeant, with a cry of, 'Get stuck in there, will ye?' No sooner had I landed on the ground than someone kicked me in the back with all their force, and I was carried off with a suspected cracked rib.

Now the military system of those days made no allowance for illness to be treated except at the morning sick parade. I was therefore carried back to the barrack-room where I lay rigid with pain throughout the night. At six I was helped off my bunk and went through the horrors of sick parade, before I eventually came face to face with Dogface.

I say face to face, but in fact I entered the room bent double, since this was the only position which would ease my pain.

Dogface's greeting was typical. 'Didn't they teach you to stand to attention when speaking to an officer?' he snarled at me.

I explained that I had been kicked in the back playing rugby. This was particularly untactful, because Dogface was a hockey maniac, who hated the officer in charge of rugby.

'That,' he said severely, 'is your own fault for playing such a stupid game. Medicine and duty. Now get out.'

I crawled out and returned to duty. It is, however, not easy being a soldier when you have to go round bent double and it wasn't long before my peculiar shape was noticed by various N.C.O.'s. Any explanation, however, was useless, since the M.O. had passed me as fit, and from the Army's point of view I was therefore in perfect health. Eventually, after trying to do rifle drill bent at right angles, I was hauled up before the Commanding Officer.

The evidence was given by my troop corporal. It would not have stood up against cross-examination by Sir Norman Birkett, but in military terms it was sufficient. 'This man,' said the corporal, 'has been lazy, idle and dozey on parade, sah. He is a lazy-dozey-idle-man sah.'

'This is a pretty poor show, Green,' said the C.O. 'I can well believe the corporal. Look at you man, you can't even be bothered to stand up straight when speaking to an officer.'

Experience of the Army had taught me the value of silence. I maintained a glassy stare at the floor.

'You're just not pulling your weight,' said the Major.

'Two hours extra rifle drill every night for a week. And for God's sake stand up straight, man. You look like a bloody praying mantis.'

Fate came to my aid. Trying to keep up with the sergeant's maniacal barkings as I was marched away, I stumbled on the stairs and sprained my ankle. As they had to cut away my boot to get it off, even Dogface could not ignore the swelling and I was reluctantly put on light duties, which meant picking up pieces of paper with a spike. By the time the ankle had healed, the ribs had too.

Fortunately, Dogface vanished soon afterwards. He developed an obsession about impetigo and kept painting everyone's face with a horrid green liquid. The Commanding Officer became tired of being in charge of 500 green-faced men and Dogface was posted. But to this day my first instinct on entering a doctor's surgery is to stand to attention and remove my trousers automatically.

Y is for . . .

Yellow-belly

Despite the fact that rugby is supposed to be a game for the fit and strong in body and spirit, most rugby teams have their quota of yellow-bellies, or full-blooded cowards. In the lower echelons whole teams may be composed of loud-mouthed cravens, shouting for someone else to 'tackle man, tackle' as they pant round a suburban field.

Yellow-bellies even infiltrate to the highest levels, and the average international side usually has one or even two, although they are frequently skilful enough to disguise the fact. The superb footwork of many a top-class stand-off has been developed not as an attacking weapon, but because the player is scared stiff of being caught by the wing-forwards.

Standards of courage, of course, are higher at the international level and what might be quite acceptable for the Extra First won't do for Wales. Outside of the first team falling on the ball isn't compulsory. If you can do it, so much the better, but if you prefer to fly-kick wildly you won't lose your place. After all, the skipper is probably doing the same sort of thing, although this won't stop him bellowing, 'Fall, damn you, fall,' on every possible occasion.

The philosophy of rugby is rather peculiar in its attitude to cowardice, which is considered the ultimate sin, while mere inefficiency, which is much more dangerous, is considered excusable.

The worst thing that can be said of a player is that he lacks guts, but this is a false belief. I have seen far more matches lost by players who lacked intelligence than by men who lacked guts.

It is considered unforgivable to shirk a tackle, but quite excusable to run wildly at the runner and fall over when he sidesteps. Similarly, any man who refuses to fall on the ball is sub-human, but someone who falls on the wretched thing, refuses to get off it and gives away a penalty which loses the match suffers little, if any, criticism.

The biggest coward I knew was a lad at school nick-named Piggy. Piggy was so enormous that nobody ever crossed his path on or off the field. He was something of a bully and would send battalions of younger boys to the tuckshop to bring him sweets, which he would eat in the playground, occasionally throwing one to a small boy as if he were a dog.

Piggy played for none of the school teams, but was king of his House junior side, marching down the field sur-rounded by yelping crowds of small figures, although he rarely scored as he tended to run out of breath after the first ten yards. One day, a tiny full-back, aged about 13, was left facing Piggy alone, and, weeping with sheer helpless-ness, ran at Piggy and butted him in the stomach. To every-one's astonishment Piggy sank to the ground and promptly began to blubber.

The anxious games-master enquired if he had suffered any injury in his vital parts but no, it was just that no one had dared to lay hands on him before. He was helped off the field still blubbering and from then on never played rugby again. His reign of terror also ended in the playground where he might sometimes be seen mournfully sucking bullseyes while passing boys taunted him.

Fortunately, cowards have a natural affinity for each other on the rugby field. Like homosexuals, they *know*. Speak-ing as a five-star, ocean-going coward myself, it was always a great relief to find the person opposite was not one of the bulldog breed. You can usually tell in the first tackle – it's the look in his eyes as you bore into him, the shifty, hunted glance that says, 'Let's all be pals, we don't want any rough stuff, do we?'

This is usually accompanied by a quite unnecessary pass or kick which the kicker is reluctant to follow up. Sometimes a yellow-belly will communicate more directly with his opposite number, actually smiling at him or even muttering some ingratiating sentence.

Forward cowards tend to do a lot of shouting, piling in the *back* of the rucks with great oaths, but they take great care not to be too near the ball, where all the scrapping is going on.

Full-back cowards have a wonderful sense of timing which allows them always to arrive a fraction of a second too late if someone is following up a loose ball, unless he is a coward as well. If another yellow-belly is chasing the ball, the results can be a little bizarre, with both players timing it superbly so that neither of them reach it, and then approaching in slow motion, watching each other out of the corners of their eyes.

Stand-off is sheer hell for a coward, especially if he has a funk of a scrum-half who gets rid of the ball to save himself punishment, no matter how closely the fly-half is marked. For years I played scrum-half to a man who actually used to shout 'Don't pass' as he stared with horror at the advancing wing-forwards. Not that I paid any attention – as far as I was concerned it was him or me, and fear lent fantastic length to my passes.

Perhaps it was only justice that eventually they moved *me* to stand-off (the threequarters hadn't received the ball all season), where I developed a masterly technique for missing the scrum-half's passes and making it look as if it was his fault. It took some doing, but by a clever change of pace and a body swerve, followed by a despairing groan, I could guarantee to be nowhere near the ball, no matter how good the pass was.

I think the most cowardly act I ever saw was perpetrated by a player called Galloping Jenkins, so named because of his jerky nervous run, and his habit of tossing back his long mane of hair.

Despite the fact that he had the guts of a particularly feeble rabbit, Jenkins could run, and in one game he broke right away down the wing. About twenty yards from the line

he was challenged by the full-back, a front-row forward who
had been seconded to the position for reasons which will be
understood by anyone who has played that class of rugby.
Thinking he could pass this leaden-footed oaf with ease,
Jenkins jerked away on a prancing sidestep and stuck out his
arm wildly to hand off. His outstretched fingers went
straight into the full-back's eyes and he staggered back
shouting, 'I'll get yer, yer dirty bleeder.'

This threat was reinforced by a spectator who called out
cheerfully, 'He means it too. He fractured someone's skull
last season.'

With a squawk of fear, Galloping Jenkins actually
ignored the line and turned round and ran back towards
half-way, pursued by the angry full-back. On reaching half-
way he kindly offered the ball to anyone who would take it,
but observing the snarling man-mountain moving up the
field no one would accept it. Eventually, Jenkins retreated
to his own 25, where fortunately he had the good sense to
put the ball into touch.

This however made no difference to his pursuer, who continued to chase him off the pitch and down the path. We
were playing on a local park at the time, and the full-back
returned saying he had 'chased the bastard as far as the
Great West Road, but then he escaped in the traffic.'

There was no sign of Jenkins after the match, and we
took his kit back to the clubhouse, where he arrived about
six o'clock, having had to walk three miles as he had no
money in his rugby shorts for a bus.

'...chased the bastard as far as the Great West Road'

Z is for . . .

Zebra Atkinson was one of those rugby tramps who never seem to belong to any one particular club, but who are always turning out for various teams, the sort of men who can be relied upon to have their kit with them at any given moment.

He came from the Black Country, and claimed that he once played for Walsall. I first met him in a pub near Earl's Court one Sunday lunch-time when I was going along with one of those Sunday pub sides that flourish in that area and there was Zebra, who'd just brought his kit along in case there was a game (there was, of course).

That was the afternoon he collected his nickname. I don't think I ever knew his real name, which was probably one of the outrageous Biblical titles such as Eli or Enoch which abound in the Black Country.

The two things I remember most about Zebra were his fund of Black Country stories, most of them featuring the mythical 'Aynoch' who was always suffering disaster to his most intimate organs, and his habit of addressing the opposition on the field of play.

It was this latter which led indirectly to his nickname. We were playing a team with a strong percentage of Welshmen. Now Atkinson was a stickler for the letter of the law and on catching a high punt ahead he held up his hand to the advancing Welsh forwards and said loudly, 'Give me ten yards yo Welsh boogers, ten yards or yo're all offside.'

Needless to say this appeal was ignored by the Welshmen with the result that in the showers afterwards it was discovered that Atkinson's chest, back and stomach were covered in stripes, each one representing the scraping of a Welsh boot over his prone form. Atkinson was so proud of his wounds that he insisted on showing them to the other side, some of whom believed they could identify their footprints by the peculiar nature of the studmarks ('That's mine boyo –

look, you can see where the nail's sticking out of the stud.')

His peculiar, striped appearance made it inevitable that someone should say, 'You look like a blinking zebra, man,' and from then on the nickname stuck.

I'm afraid, however, that Zebra represented everything the Rugby Union hold vile. Apart from such petty annoyances as urinating in the middle of the field, without even waiting for half-time, and his practice of referring to people's wives as 'good breeders' he had other bad habits. He was, for instance, once sent off for 'persistently taking stimulants' during a game.

He was also a menace with a lighted cigarette. Nobody minded his smoking during a game except that he never knew where the wretched thing was. He is certainly the only man I know who has set fire to a goalpost while leaning against it with a fag in his hand. One trouble was that he never stubbed them out properly, and his progress round the field would be marked by little spirals of smoke. Once he thrust a still-glowing butt end behind his ear as he plunged into a scrum, causing the hooker to rise like a rocket from the front-row with smoke pouring from his nether regions.

Naturally, Zebra was in his element on tour, where local people tended to regard him as a strange species of man-animal. His appearance in the smartest cocktail bar in Torquay must have caused a stir of interest, especially when he marched in and bellowed at the white-coated barman, ''ere, yo gie us 24 pints of yo best bitter and look slippy.'

The barman looked at Zebra as if he had just seen something unspeakably vile crawling across the floor, and replied loftily, 'We don't serve pints in this bar, sir.'

'All right,' said Zebra, 'yo gie us 48 halves then, only be quick about it, the lads'll be here in a minute.'

Zebra had a habit of acting as a sort of advance courier to the team on away matches, due to his inordinate thirst, which made him keen to get to the booze ahead of everyone else. I remember him travelling ahead of the coach on one occasion in his car, and making careful arrangements for the coach to stop at a pub on the main road where he would have all the drinks already ordered.

He stopped at the pub, and ordered sixteen pints of bitter, two shandies and three gin and tonics for the coach party. The landlord had just finished pulling the last of the pints when Zebra saw the coach approaching. He rushed outside in time to watch it vanish down the road at 50 miles an hour.

Apparently there were two pubs with the same name and the coach-driver knew only one of them. Anyway, Zebra never turned up for the kick-off, but he did put in an appearance about ten o'clock when he explained the delay by saying, 'Well, it takes a long time to drink 16 pints, not to mention the gin and tonics . . .'

We were sorry to lose Zebra, but he left us after six eventful months, in rather unusual circumstances. We had a full side for once, Zebra turned up late for the kick-off, and we borrowed someone from the touch-line, so when he turned up there wasn't room.

When Zebra arrived, surrounded by beer fumes, he shouted from the touch-line for the spare man to come off and let him come on. His request was, naturally, refused.

'Come on, yo mardy basket,' shouted Zebra, 'let's have yo off the field and me on. Yo'll never get any ball in them line-outs way yo playing.'

There was still no reply. 'I'll give yo one last chance,' bellowed Zebra. 'Him or me.'

Still no reply from the skipper. Whereupon Zebra solemnly turned his grip upside down and emptied his kit all over the touch-line.

'Damned if I'll ever play this bloody game again', he shouted.

His kit was still there at the end of the match and we took it in. We never saw Zebra again but as every item in his kit had been borrowed and never returned were able to split up his kit among the original owners.